D0984732

THE CREATION OF MEANING
IN CLINICAL SOCIAL WORK

THE CREATION OF MEANING
IN CLINICAL SOCIAL WORK

Carolyn Saari, Ph.D.

THE GUILFORD PRESS
New York • London

© 1991 The Guilford Press
A Division of Guilford Publications, Inc.
72 Spring Street, New York, NY 10012

Printed in the United States of America

This book is printed on acid-free paper.

Last digit is print number: 9 8 7 6 5 4 3 2 1

Library of Congress Cataloging-in-Publication Data

Saari, Carolyn.
    The creation of meaning in clinical social work / Carolyn Saari.
      p. cm.
    Includes bibliographical references and index.
    ISBN 0-89862-772-9
    1. Social case work—Psychological aspects. 2. Psychiatric social
work. 3. Clinical sociology. I. Title.
    [DNLM: 1. Ego. 2. Models, Theoretical. 3. Social work,
Psychiatric.   WM 30.5 S112c]
HV43.S125 1991
361.3'2—dc20
DNLM/DLC
for Library of Congress   91-24651
                                      CIP

Acknowledgments

Relationships, that is, the meanings that our interactions with other human beings come to have for us, are undoubtedly the most important possessions that any of us can have. It is inconceivable that any human creation, even if it is of limited significance, could come into existence without a number of important relationships being involved in the process of its construction. It is, of course, never possible to provide credit to all individuals who have contributed through the provision of support or the stimulation of ideas or opportunities, but there are always those whose special contributions to a particular work require an acknowledgment of gratitude.

I have long admired Jean Sanville for her special qualities as a clinician, a writer, a teacher, and a human being. It was, therefore, a great honor that she was instrumental in my being invited to speak at the California Society for Clinical Social Work's Conference on Meaning: Play, Culture and Creativity, which took place on Maui, Hawaii, in October, 1988. The conference itself was a special experience with combined professional and personal pleasures from which I gained much encouragement for continuing my work in the area of meaning. In particular, Jean's input into my ideas, which came both through her formally presented discussion of my paper and through more informal discussions, has been invaluable.

It was a former student, Sheila Healy, who first called Katherine Nelson's work to my attention. I admit, however, to not having devoted sufficient study to Nelson's work until Cynthia Stone suggested I read her work and obtained a copy of one of her books for me. The opportunity to participate in the Narrative Study Group at the College of Associated Health Professions at the University of Illinois at Chicago led by Suzanne Poirier also provided much stimulation and information.

A number of colleagues read parts of the book and/or provided helpful feedback on the material. Prominent among these individuals has been Martha Chescheir, whose friendship and special expertise in the concepts of both Sullivan and the British object relations school has been very helpful. Joseph Palombo, who has served in the last 10 years as my most severe critic, my greatest supporter, and a valued companion in excursions into the world of ideas, has also been very important. Friendly professional debates with Gerald Schamess have always enriched my clinical understanding. Others whose feedback was useful include Cynthia Stone, Natalie Holzman, and Roger Miller.

My associates at Loyola University of Chicago have been especially important in the production of this book. Many of the ideas in the book were developed or refined in the context of interactions with doctoral students in a course on meaning. A number of fellow faculty members provided stimulation and support in almost endless ways. Martha Urbanowski, however, was exceptionally helpful in reading the entire manuscript and suggesting ways of refining my often awkward expressions. Mary Schlitz, in her wonderfully organized and cooperative manner, made sure I was provided with the clerical supports I needed. Dean Charles O'Reilly and the university administration granted me time in the form of a leave of absence without which the work could not have been completed.

Sharon Panulla, my editor at the Guilford Press, has been very pleasant, supportive, and helpful in providing feedback about the writing as well as assistance in the production of the manuscript.

Last, but hardly least, Susan McDaniels has given me support in a wide variety of ways, not the least of which was arranging for my own personal transitional object to oversee the writing.

Contents

IV. CONCLUSION

I MEANING AND CAUSATION IN CLINICAL SOCIAL WORK THEORY

1 Introduction

Although clinical social work has its own values, goals, and traditions, it has never relied on any one theory. Instead, social work has drawn knowledge freely from whatever sources seemed relevant and useful. This has, of course, left the profession open to many disagreements about varying schools of thought. The disagreements often seem related more to the theoretical frameworks used to understand practice than to aspects of the practice itself. Frequently social workers have been regarded, and have regarded themselves, as better practitioners than theoreticians and as having a "practice wisdom" (Scott, 1990), and there has been more agreement about this than about the frameworks for understanding and explaining the practice.

The formal study of human behavior, including its meanings, motivations, and social contexts, is actually a relatively new field of endeavor. It is, therefore, not in the least surprising that its theory should still be in a fairly primitive state, with much yet to learn. From this perspective the adoption of any particular theoretical paradigm as a final or finished product for social work clinicians would appear to be very premature indeed. The dialogue between adherents of differing theoretical positions has ultimately contributed to a process of examination, criticism, and refinement in which the conceptual fit between the theory and the data from clinical experience has gradually improved. It is important that this process of improving the theoretical fit continue even if it is clear in advance that a perfect fit and a perfect theory are presently, and perhaps perpetually, impossible to achieve.

There are currently many competing perspectives within social work, most intentionally conceptualized at a level close to practice in order to provide the clinician with guidance in the selection of specific intervention methodology. Such perspectives are, of course, necessary. However, within the last several decades there have been quite remarkable changes in thinking in such fields as philosophy, linguistics, sociology, and child development. These new developments have been relatively slow in impacting on social work theory, but this is now beginning to occur. To date, there is reason to be optimistic about the possibility that these newer ideas can provide a general framework that will be conducive to a further explication of traditional social work practice wisdom. While the newer perspectives may provide social work with a more highly articulated framework for practice, the broader context needs to be revised before questions relative to specific clinical technique can be addressed—or perhaps even imagined.

This book is an attempt to create a revised theoretical framework for clinical social work through an integration of some of the newer ideas with the older practice wisdom that maintains traditional social work perspectives, such as the social nature of humanity and the person/situation configuration. Specifically, the theoretical framework developed here extends the ideas in *Clinical Social Work Treatment: How Does It Work?* (Saari, 1986), which proposed that treatment involves the construction of a meaning system shared by the client and the worker through which the client refines reality-processing skills that can subsequently be utilized outside the treatment situation. Here it is proposed that a conceptualization of treatment involving meaning provides a bridge between the person and the social structure as well as one between the interpersonal and the intrapsychic.

The perspective taken in this book asserts that the adaptive point of view has provided an inadequate foundation for clinical social work theory. A theory of meaning in which psychological health is indicated by a constructed personal meaning system (or identity) that is highly differentiated, articulated, and integrated is proposed to take the place of conceptualizations about adaptation. This theory of meaning, which includes the idea that what the child internalizes is his or her experience with the world, is believed to hold more utility for understanding the psychological effects of phenomena such as racism and social oppression.

In the current intellectual climate, which involves much debate between treatment methodologies based upon scientific empiricism and those based on hermeneutics, this book argues that clinical theory must rely on both a causal, developmental science and on a theory of meaning involving the narrative construction of the possible. This perspective is developed through defining *self* as the processes that underlie the capacity to create meaning, and *identity* as the content of the individual's meaning system. It is then proposed that self must be understood primarily through a developmental, causal framework, while identity is understood to involve meaning and the narrative construction of the possible. Treatment thus addresses both self and identity differentially depending upon the client's level of development and the treatment format utilized.

Motivation, Meaning, and Causation

Sigmund Freud's work, although controversial from the beginning, has provided the basic paradigm underlying treatment theory in all the clinical disciplines. Although there have been numerous challenges to a variety of aspects of classical drive theory, it has been this formulation to which most attempts at refinement have been addressed. As a result, some basic assumptions underlying Freud's theoretical formulations have remained in many approaches. Some of these assumptions are currently in need of revision from the perspective of knowledge gleaned in the 20th century. Freud proposed a unified theory of human behavior by positing the drives as the underlying motivators of behavior, the individual's meaning system, and the causation of psychopathology all at the same time. However, it is now clear that the failure to separate these three elements for differential consideration has led to some fundamental problems in treatment theory.

Although formulations of motivation have dominated the field of psychology for the last century, this concept appears to remain the most problematic. Much of the preoccupation with motivation has come from the hope that an adequate theory would make it possible to predict human behavior. If it were possible to understand what motivates people to behave in given ways, not only could the sometimes troublesome element of uncertainty be eliminated from human interactions but also certain destructive behaviors might be eliminated altogether. However, current experience indicates that clinicians are no better at predicting future behavior than are nonprofessionals who have access to the same information. Treatment expertise does not include the ability to predict the future.

Motivation and intention, which refers to the individual's understanding of what he or she wishes to do and which properly be-
longs to the realm of meaning, must be understood as different.
The concept of motivation seeks to explain why people behave as
they do and, as such, assumes that something is *driving* the person.
For this reason, approaching human behavior from the perspective
of motivation normally involves the assumption that there is a
physiologic base to psychological phenomena. While such a base
undoubtedly does exist, the fact that the specific mind–body connections are not yet fully understood often leaves such theorizing
at a philosophic, rather than at the presumed physiologic, level
(Reiser, 1984).

Lichtenberg (1989) is probably the most recent theorist to attempt a comprehensive formulation of motivation as a direct link
between physiology and behavior. He expands the number of factors involved in motivation from Freud's dualistic notions of sexuality and aggression and posits five motivational systems: (1) the
need for psychic regulation of physiological requirements, (2) the
need for attachment/affiliation, (3) the need for exploration and
assertion, (4) the need to react aversively through antagonism or
withdrawal, and (5) the need for sensual enjoyment and sexual
excitement.

Understanding the link between physiology and behavior is a
legitimate area for further study, and Lichtenberg's contribution in
this area seems useful. However, Lichtenberg is not explicit regarding the precise interaction of these factors in the individual, and
even his expanded list of motivational factors does not make prediction possible. In addition, it is likely that Lichtenberg's list of
factors influencing behavior is not complete. Stern (1985) indicated that there are so many factors involved in human behavior
that no theory of motivation to date has been able to encompass
them; this view is undoubtedly still valid.

Freud's basic assumption was that it is the unconscious content
of the mind that determines behavioral choice. Thus, Freud actually posited meaning as a variable intervening between motivation
and behavior; he understood the primary content of the unconscious to be a derivative of the drives and therefore biologically
determined. Current knowledge, however, contradicts the idea of
inherited meaning (Piaget, 1962), a theoretical change that requires
more revision of clinical theory than has frequently been appreciated.

Although an understanding of basic biological functioning is
important for social workers, it is not the central expertise utilized

in clinical social work treatment. Similarly, the ability to predict behavior is not critical to clinical social work treatment. For these reasons, the issue of motivation, understood as the biological basis for human behavior, will not be given major attention in the present work.

It is important to note, however, that in order to connect his theory of motivation with both behavior and treatment, Freud did have to interpose a theory of meaning. The area of meaning is central to clinical social work treatment. In *Clinical Social Work Treatment: How Does It Work?* I (Saari, 1986) proposed that treatment had to do with the creation, modification, and maintenance of a meaning system that could serve as a platform from which the client could make determinations about behavioral choices. It was thought that a sort of therapeutic culture was created and shared by the therapist and the client. This therapeutic culture was called the "concordance" and was seen as being central to the efficacy of the treatment itself: "Treatment works through the construction of a therapeutic concordance within which the client and the clinician, in their working alliance, practice and refine reality-processing skills which the client later can utilize in cultures external to the concordance itself" (Saari, 1986, p. 213).

It is no doubt true that there are a few instances in which a clinical social worker can help to reverse in a direct manner the cause of a client's problem. However, these instances normally involve rather simple problems. Most of the time, treatment does not work through a direct reversal of the causes of the client's problem. It is not uncommon for the clinical social worker to see a client many years after the identified problem first began. Frequently, neither the client nor the social worker can know in any objective fashion precisely what has caused the problem. In many instances, such as in dealing with the adult sequelae of childhood abuse, it is simply not possible, even if the cause is known, to alter the unfortunate experiences that caused the problem.

As Freud pointed out many years ago, behavior is multidetermined, meaning that there is, in fact, never only one cause for a problem. It is not sufficient to think in terms of simple linear causation; problems in human functioning most often have multiple roots and causes. It would be difficult indeed to do clinical treatment if it depended upon the systematic identification and elimination of all of these multiple factors. Instead of dealing directly with the cause of the problem, social work treatment works through the provision of a more adequate meaning system within which the client can cope with his or her current life. A theory of meaning would, therefore, necessarily be fundamental to an understanding of clinical social work treatment.

In recent years psychoanalysis has increasingly seen itself as involving a theory of meaning, but in that discipline this has led to a heated debate about whether the theory underlying psychoanalysis is fundamentally hermeneutic or scientific. The recognition that meaning is not biologically inherited has forced a confrontation with the fact that there are major differences between interpretive and causally oriented ways of thinking. Bruner (1986), for example, has recently observed that there are two different basic modes of human thinking. one mode of thinking has to do with causality and scientific prediction whereas the other is related to meaning and the narrative construction of the possible.

Since it has already been pointed out that clinical social work treatment does not often work through the direct reversal of the causes of the client's presenting problem, it is possible to take the position that clinical social work is exclusively a hermeneutic discipline and does not need to deal with the scientific mode of thought. Bruner, however, pointed out that in everyday life the two modes of thought are used in an interrelated fashion. Clinical treatment can be thought of as seeking to develop in or restore to the client ways of thinking and coping that are ordinarily thought of as characteristic of everyday life. Thus, it would seem reasonable that a theory of clinical treatment might encompass the use of both modes of thought.

There is an intuitive appeal to the idea that treatment theory involves both kinds of thinking. This possibility fits with Holt's (1976) observation that in trying to develop a theory that would be purely scientific, Freud invented an elaborate framework that increasingly seemed to have less and less relationship to the clinical data. Klein (1976) pointed out that Freud's work actually contained two separable theories—one related to clinical data or meaning and a second composed of the metapsychological explanations. Thus, both causal thinking and the narrative construction of the possible may always have been necessary for treatment theory. In saying that both developmental and clinical theory are necessary to an understanding of treatment but need to be separated from each other, Palombo (1989b) seems to have been making a similar point.

The definition of clinical social work utilized in my earlier work (Saari, 1986) stated that clinical social work treatment is both an art and a science:

The goal of clinical social work is the improvement of social functioning through the enhancement of the meaningfulness of life experiences and an expansion of the range of choices for individual behavior in an environment capable of supporting a variety of adaptive patterns. This goal rests upon the foundation of a belief in the dignity of all human beings and the necessity for a communal responsibility for all members of society. Services provided may be geared toward the prevention of future difficulties, toward more effective coping with current situations, toward the stabilization of achieved coping capacities, and/or toward remediation for the effects of stresses from the past. While the individual as a biopsychosocial system remains a basic unit of concern, persons may be served alone, in families, or in small groups.

The practice of clinical social work involves a process in which assessment, goal setting, planned intervention, and evaluation are prominent features. The effectiveness of the interventions is presumed to rely upon the strengthening and reordering of the organizational structures in the client's life, including those structures that have traditionally been seen as intrapsychic, interpersonal, institutional, and/or societal. Practice invariably takes place in the context of a purposeful relationship within which the tools selected for intervention may involve available and appropriate social resources as well as the professional self of the social worker. The practice of clinical social work is neither an art nor a science, since such a division is artificial—it is both. (p. 12)

Presumably, clinical social work also involves the realms of both meaning and causation.

In recent years there have been many attempts to examine of treatment efficacy from the point of view of a causal science. Yet such research-based attempts have generally failed to capture the essence of the treatment endeavor, which has often been sacrificed in favor of scientific rigor. On the other hand, most clinicians are not comfortable with the idea that treatment is such an individual and artistic enterprise that there can be no basis on which to evaluate its efficacy. A perspective involving both the realm of meaning and the realm of causal science seems necessary.

Yet meaning and causation do seem to be quite different ways of conceptualizing and do employ different problem-solving strategies. Understanding that both are involved in theory for clinical social work treatment means that an exploration of how each of these types of thinking is utilized in treatment and of the nature of the relationship between them is essential for the further development of treatment theory.

Relationship as the Meaning of Interaction

Throughout the history of clinical social work the client–therapist relationship has been considered a critical factor for therapeutic outcome. During the 1940s and 1950s virtually every major social work theoretician discussed the concept of relationship. This theme was so extensive that Perlman (1979) suggested that it may have been "discussed to death." In 1957 Biestek observed that the importance of the relationship was universally recognized and called the relationship "the soul of social casework." In a recent introduction to a volume on various theoretical approaches to clinical social work, Ann Hartman (1988) notes that although there are broad differences between the points of view represented, all have in common the perspective of the person-in-situation and the view that change takes place within the context of a relationship.

The emphasis on the client–therapist relationship and its use in treatment has traditionally been one of the most distinctive features of a social work approach to therapy. In spite of this emphasis, however, social work theorists have generally not been able to specify the precise manner in which the relationship leads to a therapeutic outcome. Typically, social work authors have either satisfied themselves with a description of the characteristics of a therapeutic relationship or simply relied on references to humanitarian values. For example, in *Relationship: The Heart of Helping People*, Perlman (1979) lists warmth, acceptance, caring concern, and genuineness as necessary qualities of the helping relationship. Although she raises the issue of the effects of the relationship, her discussion becomes more vague at this point and generally expresses to the idea that a helping relationship is important in the promotion of learning.

Perlman notes that a helping relationship is a necessary but not sufficient condition for a therapeutic outcome, a position that probably represents the opinions of most social work theoreticians. The relationship is seen as the *context* of the treatment but not the essence of the treatment. Yet Perlman does note that in some instances the achievement of a relationship may be the goal of the treatment. Other social work theoreticians, who are reluctant to adopt the term *transference* from psychoanalysis and who seem to mean something technically different, frequently utilize the phrase "therapeutic use of the self" (or sometimes "conscious use of the self") to designate their understanding of the interactive process in traditional casework.

During the 1960s, with the optimism that accompanied the inception of the poverty programs, there was an attempt to translate the idea of a helping relationship into the substitution of self-help groups and paraprofessionals for the more expensive and less available clinician with training. It was, after all, obvious that trained clinicians had no monopoly on the commodity of legitimate caring. Since the clinicians had not specified precisely how the self was differentially used in a therapeutic manner by someone with professional training, it was simply not evident to social planners that such training was necessary. Clinicians did not have a readily available theory to explain the therapeutic efficacy of a professional relationship, and they were themselves both frustrated and open to charges of wishing to perpetuate a kind of elitism or professional privilege.

The questions that arose concerning the efficacy of social work treatment during the 1960s resulted to some extent from instances of treatment that seemed to ramble on endlessly without defined goals. Clinicians clearly could not reasonably defend such practices. Since the state of theory relative to the use of a helping relationship was primitive at best, behaviorist, task-centered, and other techniques that could be made more explicit and definable came into fashion. Although the behavior theorists initially attempted to ignore or dismiss the variable of relationship as of no consequence, the demands of practice soon led this group of clinicians back to the necessity of considering the role of the relationship (Margolen & Goldman, 1974; Schwartz and Goldiamond, 1975).

In the past, clinical social work theorizing has not normally made a distinction between interaction and relationship. Stern (1989a) points out that an interaction is an interpersonal event as externally viewed whereas a relationship is the interaction along with its subjective interpretation. Thus, a relationship always involves the meaning attached by the participant(s) to the interaction involved. An interaction, therefore, may be discussed in a framework involving causal science, but a relationship resides in the realm of meaning.

The Social Construction of Meaning

One of clinical social work's traditional imperatives has been "start where the client is." In accordance with this dictum the social worker is expected to elicit the client's understanding of his or her problem, to relate to the client differentially depending on that understanding, and to utilize that understanding in the conduct of the treatment as it proceeds. "Starting where the client is" has been thought to be basic both to a professional respect for the individuality of the client and to the preservation of self-determination for the client. As such, this particular tenet of social work practice wisdom has been fundamental to the values of the profession as well as to practice methodology. Another way of stating this idea is to say that the clinical social worker deals with the client's meaning system. Professional experience, going back at least to the days of Mary Richmond (1917), indicates that what matters in determining the client's problem-solving behavior is not necessarily the situation in which the client finds himself or herself as viewed from a purely external or objective point of view. Instead, it is the manner in which the client construes that situation that is of special significance. In retrospect, it appears that the reason social work theorists became interested in psychoanalysis during the 1920s had to do with the hope of finding a way of better comprehending the manner in which the client's meaning system was constructed and in which it then influenced behavior.

The idea of meaning has always been central to psychoanalytic theory. Indeed, Freud's (1900) earliest psychoanalytic writing concerned an understanding of the meaning of dream material. While Freud, too, was interested in explaining human behavior, he approached this from a perspective somewhat different from that of most social workers today. Since his work centered on understanding neuroses and pathology, he focused on the possible origins of intrapsychic conflict rather than on the manner in which the individual acquires an understanding of a particular problem or situation. This emphasis led Freud somewhat away from the focus on the interaction between the person and the situation, a focus that most interests social workers. Thus, while Freud's theory offers clinical social workers some valuable insights and considerable hope for further knowledge, it has always had identifiable and seemingly inherent limitations.

Freud was very much aware of and influenced by the science of his day. He was preceded by Darwin by only a few decades, and evolution was the predominant model for theorizing. Thus, Freud believed that unconscious symbols were basically primitive and constituted a sort of inherited ancient language through which ontogeny recapitulated phylogeny in each individual in every culture (Litowitz & Litowitz, 1977). Freud believed that there were symbols in the unconscious, uniform for all people, that represented such concepts as immediate blood relatives, birth, death and love. Ultimate meaning, therefore, was biologically inherited.

Underlying Freud's approach and that of his contemporaries, however, was a static conception of the external world and of the human being's interaction with it. The psychoanalytic concept of "reality testing," long a favorite with social workers, is an excellent example. Freud defined the ability to test reality as the capacity to know if a given stimulus was coming from the internal world of the psyche or from the external world. It was simply assumed that a constant and accurate perception of the external world was not only possible but was readily available to the healthy person (Schimek, 1975). In 1974 Robbins and Sadow pointed out that there is much more to an understanding of the external world than what was meant by the term *reality testing* and proposed that psychoanalysis adopt the term *reality processing* for the cognitive skills involved. An even more current way of describing what human beings actually do would be "reality constructing."

The philosophy of science now achieving dominance basically involves a constructivist approach to cognition (Watzlawick, 1984). Constructivism stands in stark contrast to the earlier logical positivist stance that the truth could be known only through direct observation. Instead, constructivism holds that no data, no observation, has meaning in and of itself but must be interpreted within a created theoretical framework. Human beings are understood to have only mediated, not direct, knowledge of the world (Polanyi & Prosch, 1975). The knowledge that any observation yields is totally dependent upon the lens through which the observation is made (Bronowski, 1978).

Watzlawick (1984) has compared the human situation in relation to knowledge of the world to that of the sea captain who must sail through uncharted waters where there is a reef. If the ship happens to pass through the area without hitting the reef, the captain now knows where the reef is not—but not where it is. If the ship founders, the captain knows where the reef is but still does not know where it is not. A series of trips through such waters yields a better picture—but never a totally accurate one. Mapmakers may later make use of this captain's, and many other captains', experiential knowledge to create a map from which the traveler can understand the passage through the reef. Such a map will be useful for sailing through these waters and will certainly be more accurate than if it were based on the information from only one trip through the reef, but it is not possible for the map to be absolutely complete and correct. Even apart from the measurement problems, which are considerable, the tides mean that the reef will have changed since the last trip.

We human beings cannot achieve a God's-eye view of the world. As the French psychoanalyst Jacques Lacan (1973) has noted, even in our dreams, where we are the sole authors of the story, we do not see everything at once but must instead wait for the tale to unfold. We are, nevertheless, fundamentally meaning-makers, so that from even very early in life we create hypotheses about the nature of the world around us (Stern, 1985). In fact, we are such inveterate meaning-makers that when we do not have an explanation for something, we make one up. We cling to that explanation, even if we know it is incorrect, until such time as we can find or create a more satisfying explanation.

Although criticisms of Freud's idea of an inherited unconscious symbolic system do not seem to appear in the psychoanalytic literature until the 1950s (Rycroft, 1956), this idea is no longer consonant with knowledge from several disciplines and has been disavowed by most psychoanalytic theorists. Instead, current thinking is more in concert with the philosopher Heidegger (1927), who pointed out that truth exists neither in the mind of the knower nor in the object that is known; rather, truth results from an interaction between the two. It appears, however, that meaning results not from such a two-party interaction but from one involving three—the knower, the known, and another human being who might best be called a sharer (Werner & Kaplan, 1963). Thus, the construction of meaning is fundamentally an interpersonal process.

Current theories outside of social work are now suggesting both that meaning is created in interpersonal interaction and that the content of the meaning system of the individual is basically reflective of that person's experiences in an environment that is both social and physical. The concept of a created meaning, however, calls into question the traditional psychoanalytic understanding of interpretation as the curative element in treatment. Indeed, much of the progress in clinical theories in recent years has directed the clinician's attention away from the perspective that the therapeutic effect derives directly from the accuracy of the therapist's specific interpretations. The more recent formulations have focused on process factors in the therapeutic interaction, rather than only on the content of what is literally said.

If there are no unconscious symbols that have universal meaning, then the therapist's role cannot be that of providing a translation for the client of the underlying meaning of the symbols in his or her unconscious life. Furthermore, if there is no final correct or objective view of the world, then the therapist cannot be thought of as able to provide a sort of undistorted truth for the client either. Clearly, interpretation cannot be viewed as having either of these functions in treatment. However, interpretation can also be considered to be a process involving the creation of meaning (Saari, 1988). It is from this point of view that I previously proposed that treatment involved a process in which meaning was created in the interactions between client and clinician (Saari, 1986).

One of the implications of the supposition that treatment involves an interpersonal process in which meaning is created is that some individuals may be more capable of participating in that process than others. In other words, some individuals may have difficulty forming a relationship involving the creation of meaning out of human interaction. These individuals would then be seen as having a deficit in the capacity to create meaning, and a major goal of the treatment would appropriately be to enhance or further develop that capacity.

If the clinical social worker is to know how to enhance the capacity to create meaning, attention needs to be paid to such questions as the following: How does the capacity to create meaning normally develop?; What conditions or events would interfere in its development?; and How can the interpersonal interactions in treatment be converted to a relationship in order to stimulate growth in this capacity? These questions seem to fall into the realm of a developmental and a causal science.

On the other hand, one cannot practice or refine the capacity to create meaning in a vacuum of meaning content. Interpretation, in the sense of a process involving the creation of meaning, is potentially infinite. Any number of meanings could be constructed about client behaviors or verbalizations. How, then, does a therapist make a choice as to which possible meanings might be formulated within treatment? Are there guidelines concerning which meanings might be more useful to a client than others? And if the therapist does participate actively with the client in the creation of meaning, how can the principle of self-determination be preserved rather than impose the social worker's meaning system on the client? These questions fall more clearly into the realm of the narrative construction of the possible.

2 The Interpersonal and the Intrapsychic

In the past, theories about psychotherapy have tended to be considered either intrapsychic or interpersonal. In the current practice environment in which individual, couple, family, and group treatment all appear to have some effectiveness, the need is for a theory that can encompass both intrapsychic phenomena and the interpersonal world while providing a basis for understanding their fundamental interrelatedness. The treatment situation itself, no matter which of the aforementioned modalities is used, is fundamentally interpersonal. Yet, at least in accordance with the idea that treatment works through the construction, maintenance, and/or reorganization of the client's meaning system, this interpersonal situation is utilized to effect change in an intrapsychic one.

Currently, it is not unusual for the use of the rather impersonal term *object* in object relations theory to be explained on the basis of a subject–object differentiation. This is not, however, the true origin of the term. Freud specified that the instinctual drives had four characteristics: (1) a source, which was generally physiologic; (2) an impetus or strength; (3) an aim, which for the libidinal drive was sexual union; and (4) an object, which for the libidinal drive was normally the opposite sex. Thus, the very notion of social interaction entered psychoanalytic theory only through a sort of back door as a requisite characteristic of an instinctual drive (Greenberg & Mitchell, 1983).

Freud (1923) stated that the character of the ego was the precipitate of abandoned object-cathexes and that it contained the history of these object-choices. Yet this statement implies a much more specified notion of the importance of others in human life than

16

Freud actually outlined in his theoretical formulations and is probably so frequently quoted because of its implication that he would
not have opposed such a theory. Although Freud implied that the
object had some relationship to ego development, he left the nature of this relationship rather vague. What actually is an object-
cathexis and of what does the precipitate consist? Freud did not
develop ideas about the precise relationship between the development of the psychic functioning of one human being and social
contact with another human being.

In his clinical writing Freud gave detailed descriptions of his
patients' intimate relationships, yet he often seems incredibly naive
to the modern reader about the clinical implications of these relationships. The most extreme example of this is seen in the Dora
case, where Freud (1905) failed to understand the possible effect of
a father's bringing his daughter for treatment even though he
seems to have been aware that the father's motivation was at least
partly to ease the complications of his daughter's behavior on his
own extramarital affair. In the same case Freud seems to have
thought it both strange and pathologic that a physically normal 18-
year-old girl would refuse the sexual attentions of a reasonably
attractive middle-aged man. The complicated web of interpersonal
relationships, including the fact that this man was the husband of
the girl's father's mistress, seems not to have been considered by
Freud sufficient reason for a normal girl to wish to decline sexual
involvement. Freud clearly expected that instinctual drive, as compared to the nature of the interpersonal relationships, would have
a primary influence over behavior.

Although object relations theorists since Freud have moved in
the direction of a more interpersonal theory, it has not been until
recently that this has been unreservedly so, at least within the
mainstream of American psychoanalytic thinking. For example,
Mahler (Mahler, Pine, & Bergman, 1975), whose work has been
highly influential in the United States, considered her theory a
formulation of the development of the child's intrapsychic structure. Although she detailed the interactions between mother and
child, Mahler repeatedly warned that an instinctual or genetic
inheritance would ultimately have the most significant influence
over the long-range result. Thus, although much of the clinical
social work community has utilized Mahler's theory as if it were an
interpersonal one, it was not actually intended as such and technically became so only through an extension of the instinctual back
door in Freudian theory.

In a similar sense, there has been a tendency on the part of many clinical social workers to interpret Kohut's notion of the "self-object" as being an interpersonal concept. Yet a careful reading of Kohut's work indicates that Kohut himself was ambivalent at best about such a possible interpretation. This may have been part of the reason that it was not until his final work, actually published after his death, that Kohut (1984) indicated his belief that healthy human beings need selfobjects throughout their lives. Even so, Goldberg (1988), the most prominent of the self psychologists now maintaining a strict interpretation of Kohut's work, is adamant that the selfobject concept refers to the function of the other person for intrapsychic functioning and is therefore not an interpersonal concept.

If, however, Kohut was ambivalent about the notion of an interpersonally based psychodynamic theory, Daniel Stern, who has professed himself to be most influenced by self psychology, certainly has not been. Indeed even the title of his book, *The Interpersonal World of the Infant*, signaled a different approach in psychoanalytic theory. Stern (1985) declared, "Another way to put all of this is that the infant's life is so thoroughly social that most of the things the infant does, feels, and perceives occur in different kinds of relationships" (p. 118). Stern's work is currently receiving considerable acceptance within psychoanalytic circles, a development that should be encouraging to social workers who have traditionally taken a more interpersonal stance.

Stern was not, of course, the first psychoanalyst to imply an interpersonal point of view. Although not usually labeled as interpersonal, Jacobson's (1964) description of object representations is clearly an attempt at an explanation of the manner in which interpersonal interaction affects the development of an inner life. Similarly, Melanie Klein's (1964) theory of object relations emphasizes the influence of the mother. Currently Klein's concept of projective identification in which the individual assigns an aspect of the self to the interacting partner yet retains an identification with that aspect, has become a popular means for understanding the manner that interaction, such as occurs in the treatment situation (Ogden, 1982), can affect the intrapsychic experience of the interactive partners.

Winnicott (1958b), who was heavily influenced by Klein but thought her ideas insufficiently interpersonal, believed it was important to think of the mother and child as an originally indivisible unit. Much of his work centered on the development of a sense of self out of this original unity. For example, Winnicott believed that it was not possible to retain a sense of self either in isolation from others or when psychologically fused with another human being. Thus, from this perspective, the maintenance of a sense of self would require constant monitoring of the interpsychic space between persons so as to ensure optimal distance during interpersonal interactions.

The work of one more recent theorist, Hans W. Loewald (1980c), provides an important clue in gaining a perspective on the presumed intrapsychic–interpersonal controversy. Loewald was originally a student of Heidegger, as well as of Freud. Thus, much of his work has been a reinterpretation of Freud from the point of view that the "truth" lies in the interaction between the subject and the object. Loewald retained much of the orthodox psychoanalytic language, including that of the drives and instincts. But Loewald considered the instincts to be psychic forces that were actually constituted through the interaction between mother and child.

If the language of Freud's economic point of view is dropped from Loewald's work, one might then define instincts not as psychic forces but, rather, as meaning systems. It can then be said that the intrapsychic meaning system of the child is constituted through the interaction between mother and child. This statement does not constitute a major distortion in Loewald's theory and is, of course, in accord with the constructivist point of view outlined earlier.

Subjective Experience and the Self

Since Freud had assumed that the important meanings in his theory were those that were biologically inherited and were contained in the unconscious—or later, presumably, the id—his theory did not have a major emphasis on a concept similar to the *self* of current theory. From Hartmann on, however, analysts have found such a concept necessary. In part, at least, the concept of a self, usually defined as that part of the person that experiences, has been necessary because Freud's attempts to achieve a scientific theory resulted in formulations of the id, ego, and superego that were so mechanized that the subjective experience of the individual seemed excluded from consideration.

While the current psychoanalytic school referred to as *self psychology* was begun by Kohut (1984), it now seems to have united a number of theorists with somewhat different perspectives. The agreement among the diverse members of this school seems to consist of a rejection of drive theory and metapsychology in favor of a greater emphasis on the individual's subjective experience (Palombo, 1989a). The concept of the self, however, has a history outside of psychoanalysis in the work of Baldwin (1902), Cooley (1964), and Mead (1934). There are many similarities between Kohut's approach to the self and that of Mead and Cooley; since Mead was a prominent figure at the University of Chicago, where Kohut had his psychiatric training, it is quite possible that although Kohut does not credit these sources, his work may have been influenced by the symbolic interactionist school of thought with which these men are now associated.

Mead's work has had a significant influence on both clinical social work and psychiatry, partly through Sullivan's (1953) interpersonal ideas about treatment. Mead, who considered himself to be a behaviorist but was unhappy with some of the more extreme implications of Watson's (1919) ideas, formulated a theory in which both mind and meaning could be seen as developing through social interaction. Mentality was the individual's symbolically mediated awareness of those elements in the environment that respond to his or her actions. Thus, for Mead, mind did not reside in the central nervous system but in the interaction between the organism and its surround.

In Mead's theory the self is not present at birth but is developed in the individual through the process of social experience and activity. Mead pointed out that physical sensation could exist without a self. What was distinctive about the self was its ability to reflect upon itself, to take itself as an object of reflexiveness. In a way, although Mead clearly avoided utilizing terminology that implied an intrapsychic life, the concept of a self able to examine its own experience can be seen as a type of formulation about the development of consciousness.

There is still considerable controversy among child development experts as to when the self can be said to have formed. A number of authors point to developments occurring normally at around 18 months as signaling the presence of a self (Kagan, 1981; Lewis & Brooks-Gunn, 1979; Lichtenberg, 1983). On the basis of recent studies demonstrating that the young infant is in fact more competent than had previously been suspected, Stern (1985) speaks of an "emergent self" present at birth and a "core self" beginning at 2 or 3 months.

In part it appears that the differences in the age at which the self can be said to develop are semantic, dependent upon the particular behaviors or evidence chosen as definitional. On the other hand, as long as the self is defined in terms of the child's ability to have an awareness of subjective experience, there may always be some controversy about the age at which this develops. In spite of sophisticated advances in the techniques used to research infant competencies, interpreting data on the infant's subjective experiences still requires making a number of assumptions and it is difficult to conceive that it will ever be possible to know beyond question the nature of the inner life of the preverbal child.

In part, however, the more recent trend toward crediting the younger child with a self has been a result of revisions in the understanding of the relationship between affect and cognition. Previously, there was a tendency to assume, along with Freud, that affect is somehow primitive and biologically inherited whereas cognition, which is presumably more rational, develops later. Current developmentalists (Demos, 1982; Stern, 1985) are no longer seeing a split between affect and cognition as defensible; in fact, Bruner (1986) considers the previous tendency to split these as a major cause of considerable difficulty in understanding child development. That some forms of affect/cognition are present at birth is undisputed; the question therefore is clearly, At what age is the infant aware of what experiences? That is, it becomes a question of consciousness.

In his classic paper on the unconscious, Freud (1915) asked what made the difference between what was conscious and what was unconscious and decided that it was language, specifically the presence of an association between a word and the thing to which it referred, that was the critical element:

> The system Ucs. contains the thing-cathexis of the objects, the first and true object-cathexes; the system Pcs. comes about by this thing-presentation being hypercathected through being linked with the word-presentations corresponding to it. It is these hypercathexes, we may suppose, that bring about a higher psychical organization and make possible for the primary process to be succeeded by the secondary process which is dominant in the Pcs. (pp. 201–202)

Freud was relying on an associationist theory of language acquisition that is no longer acceptable to linguists. Although there is still no universally accepted theory of language acquisition, it is clear that language cannot develop without interaction with other human beings. Therefore, it might be said that Freud was implying that making the unconscious conscious was dependent on participation in human interaction.

In a discussion of the nature of the self and of its origin that draws partly upon Mead's ideas, Sroufe (1989) stresses the following:

> In brief, it will be argued that the self should be conceived as an inner organization of attitudes, feelings, expectations, and meanings, which arises from an organized caregiving matrix. That is, the dyadic infant–caregiver organization precedes and gives rise to the organization that is self. . . . The self is a social creation, and it is defined, maintained, and transformed with reference to others. (p. 71)

Sroufe does not go quite so far as to indicate that the caregiving matrix gives rise to conscious experience. On the other hand, if the ability to reflect back upon itself is considered to be the distinguishing quality of the self, it would appear that Sroufe's formulation would have to mean just that.

If one assumes, as Piaget (1962) does, that what is inherited consists of action patterns, it is perfectly possible to assume that there is a biologically inherited unconscious that has an important influence upon human behavior without assuming that this unconscious is in the form of preformulated meanings. Action patterns—and, as Mead noted, even physical sensations—can occur without the individual having the ability to reflect upon or be aware of them. This is essentially the finding of Bruch's (1969; Coddington & Bruch, 1970) studies on severe anorexia nervosa.

Werner and Kaplan (1963) agreed with Piaget that what was inherited were action patterns. However, they indicated that at some point children become capable of viewing the objects in the world around them as things-of-contemplation rather than just as things of action. For Werner and Kaplan, it is in the process of the sharing of contemplations of external objects with a significant other that the child's capacity to utilize the symbols that later undergird thought and language develops. There is, however, reason to believe that the process of sharing between a caregiver and an infant actually begins before the shared contemplation of external objects occurs.

As Stern (1985) points out, sharing in the sense of a "self-regulating other," that is, in having one's physical and affective experience partially controlled through the environment provided by the human other, begins prior to birth and continues to be a prominent aspect of experience in the early months of life. Such sharing, however, probably remains mostly at a level of unconscious action patterns throughout life. On the other hand, Stern points out, the infant learns which experiences are shareable with others, based upon those to which the caregiver becomes affectively attuned.

Stern's description of affect attunement is a theoretical contribution of critical importance. He points out that human beings experience pure imitation not as empathy at all but, rather, as mockery. In order to convey to another that we have understood his or her inner state, it is necessary for us to perform a kind of translation of the other person's affective experience into another medium or modality of expression. Stern points out that this kind of affect attunement is normally unconscious and involves what he refers to as the "vitality affects." Vitality affects are related to states of pleasure or unpleasure and involve such things as shape, intensity, motion, number, and rhythm, as well as dynamic, kinetic feelings like surging or fading away. The vitality affects are thus distinguished from the categorical affects such as mad, sad, glad, or scared.

Stern (1985) provides a number of illustrations of affect attunement and misattunement in early mother–child interactions. A typical example of attunement might be that of an infant who is enthusiastically propelling a toy automobile with a certain rhythm while the mother is vocalizing "Whee, whee" in the same rhythm that the child is using in moving the toy. Here what has occurred, in Stern's terms, is "cross-modal matching." That is, the mother has matched the child's vitality affect in another modality (here, a verbal one). Stern notes that this kind of affect attunement becomes prominent in the building of the child's intersubjective sense of self, which begins at about 7 or 8 months of life.

According to Stern, affect attunements are themselves primarily unconscious events. Mother, for example, is not normally aware that she is vocalizing in precisely the same rhythm that the child uses in moving the toy. These kinds of interactive attunements continue to occur throughout life, are the very stuff of what has generally been called unconscious nonverbal communication, and underlie perceptions of whether or not another person is empathic. Furthermore, Stern has stated, it is through attunement that the child learns what can be shared with other human beings.

While it is likely that considerable further attention through research ought to be paid to the interpersonal processes of affect attunement and its effects on psychological life, it seems reasonable to point out that those experiences that are potentially shareable with another can also be communicated (albeit perhaps imperfectly) through some medium. Such experiences then can also be seen as shareable with the self; that is, they can be the subjects of self-reflection. Furthermore, what is not potentially shareable with another (and therefore not shareable with the self, either) may remain an influential part of one's total experience—but on an unconscious level.

This line of thinking has, therefore, led to the conclusion that the self (defined, for the moment, in Mead's terms as self-reflexiveness) is a social self that arises out of interpersonal experiences with affect attunement. Conscious subjective experience is constructed out of interpersonal interactions. This conclusion, in turn, has critically important implications for understanding the role of interpersonal interactions within the processes of treatment. For if it is the individual's conscious awareness of choices that creates the possibility of improved social functioning and if it is experience with affect attunement that creates the possibility of conscious awareness, then it hardly seems surprising that a basically empathic interpersonal relationship has been found to be essential to effective treatment.

Four Functions of Meaning

The self, when defined in Mead's terms as having the distinctive ability to reflect upon itself, depends upon meaning that has been made at least potentially shareable. Certainly it is true that a conscious sense of self is critical for social functioning. It is with this capacity that the human being is able to contemplate and convey meaning as well as plan, direct, and evaluate his or her own behavior. Yet it is also true that experiences that the individual has had but that may not have become shareable may also continue to influence behavior. These experiences also have meaning, albeit perhaps unconscious, meaning that can potentially be consciously constructed. For this reason, a distinction is being made here between *meaning* (or *meaningful*), which refers generally to any experience of the individual that may have affective–cognitive significance, and *meaning system*, which refers to meaning that has been actively or consciously constructed by the person.

It should be noted that this usage is different from that apparently preferred by Stern (1985), who reserves the term *meaning* specifically for what has been constructed through language: "Meaning results from interpersonal negotiations involving what can be agreed upon as shared. And such mutually negotiated meanings (the relation of thought to word) grow, change, develop and are struggled over by two people and thus ultimately owned by *us*" (p. 170). The point here is not that meaning is not the result of interpersonal interactions or that it is not shared but, rather, that defining meaning as strictly related to language seems much too limiting and intellectualized. Indeed, it seems a contradiction within Stern's own work that he, who seems to have so carefully explained the affective-cognitive significance of the infant's early experiences, should have defined meaning in this manner.

Since Stern and many other developmentalists are now indicating that the division between affect and cognition is a false and misleading one, the term *meaning* is utilized here to refer to significance that has within it a mixture of what has previously been divided into affect and cognition. Meaning, in this sense, is an extremely important phenomenon to understand in relation to human behavior and has at least four separable but interrelated functions for the individual, namely, communication, organization, evaluation, and participation in a human community.

Communication

Nonverbal communication clearly begins at the onset of life and later coexists with communication through language, sometimes independently of the linguistic signs and sometimes intertwined with them. The fact that human infants display a series of distinct facial expressions that adults associate with emotional states and that these facial expressions are consistent regardless of the societal group into which the infant has been born was first observed by Darwin (1872). Although the nature of the internal states accompanying the newborn's facial expressions is now a matter of some controversy, it is generally accepted that these expressions serve as communicative signals to adult caretakers, who respond as if the expressions indicate particular internal states and thereby probably help the child to develop those states (Tomkins, 1963; Izard, 1977). Furthermore, although traditional theory (Spitz, 1965) dated the onset of the social smile to about 3 months of age, at which time there are some clear changes in the baby's communicative behavior, the infant can be observed to smile within the first 2 weeks of life (Demos, 1982).

Facial expressions are not, however, the only medium through which affect is communicated, even very early in life. During the intrauterine state the physiologic experience of the organism is regulated to a considerable extent by the host environment, that is, by the mother's body. According to Stern (1985), the neonate has the experience of having its affective states, such as calmness or anxiety, regulated through contact with another human being. For example, the infant's state can be either calmed or excited through interactions, probably primarily physical but often vocal as well, with a caretaking person. The experience of having one's own inner state calmed through a "self-regulating other" is undoubtedly the kind of experience Kohut had in mind in describing self-object functions.

Beyond these more basic media for interpersonal communication, of course, there is also communication through affect attunement and through the use of language, including direct reference to those affects such as mad, sad, glad, and scared that Stern refers to as categorical.

Organization

Human beings seem to have a fundamental need for a sense of ongoing organization in order to function properly, or perhaps even at all. The preservation of some kind of organized and reliable inner meaning system is so critical that humans will willingly endure almost any conditions of existence as long as they can comprehend and endorse the reasons for these conditions.

In Freud's first formulations of the defenses, he indicated that these organizational structures were formed in order to prevent unacceptable meanings from becoming conscious. Thus, for Freud, organization served defensive purposes. However, as Loewald (1980a) has pointed out, over time the theoretical emphasis has shifted so that the prominent view is now that defenses serve organizational purposes. In other words, the defenses serve to retain a sense of organization for the person. Pathology is now frequently described along Kohut's lines as "fragmentation."

As Krystal (1988) has indicated, there is a relationship between the relative degree of experienced organization of the self and affective experience. Experiencing a strong affect frequently provides a focus with which an individual can maintain a sense of organization. For example, anger or a negative affect can help someone under stress continue to function, at least for a period of time. For the schizophrenic individual, paranoia can serve this function (Blatt & Wild, 1976). Winnicott (1947) noted that while the experience of being loved breaks down boundaries, being hated creates them. He believed that hate could therefore create a sense of being centered in the self and separate from others. Indeed, Winnicott's idea was that in order to maintain a sense of self all human beings had to utilize affective experiences to maintain an optimum level of psychic distance from others; for him, either psychic fusion or psychic isolation threatened psychic survival.

There is, however, also a relationship between the intensity with which an affect is experienced and the ability of the individual to experience affect without disorganizing or fragmenting. As was noted by Zetzel (1970) in her classic paper "Depression and the Incapacity to Bear It," the ability to tolerate strong affect is variable and is an ego strength. Thus, while strong affect can help affirm self boundaries, strong affect can also disrupt the sense of self-organization if the intensity of that affect exceeds the individual's tolerance level. In other words, strong affect can either hold one together or lead to fragmentation, depending upon its intensity and duration. It is likely that affect tolerance is developed through experiences of interpersonal affect attunement.

Evaluation

In addition to functioning as a means of communication between individuals and of organizing experience, the categorical affects such as mad, sad, glad, and scared play a major role in the quality of inner experience. Although the precise inner experience accompanying the facial expressions of the newborn may be uncertain, the particular facial expression displayed by the infant consistently fits a situation in which the adult emotion associated with that facial expression would be considered appropriate. For example, the child displays a smile in circumstances in which it is conceivable that the child might be experiencing pleasure, the rage reaction when frustration appears likely, and so forth. Thus, there is initial consistency between the inner state that adults tend to presume the infant is experiencing and the communicative facial expression of the baby.

Basch (1976) has defined emotions as "subjectively experienced states and always related to a concept of self vis-à-vis some particular situation" (p. 768). He also notes that since infants have neither a well-developed sense of self nor the cognitive capacities for reflective consideration that are involved in what he defines as emotion, this type of experience cannot be attributed to infants. Emotions, as Basch describes them, therefore develop over the course of the child's maturation. This is, of course, in line with the understanding that an emotional or inner life develops over the course of the lifetime (Saari, 1986) and that it can no longer be taken for granted, as was the case in early psychoanalytic theory, that the inner experiences of all people are similar. Indeed, it would

now appear that the inner life of each individual is highly dependent upon that person's interactive experiences with affect attunement.

Basch's definition of emotions involves a concept of the self vis-
à-vis some particular situation. For example, feeling happy generally refers to the relationship between the self and some current
condition that may be either specifically identified or more globally
experienced. Although Basch does not specifically mention the
notion of evaluation, an evaluative function relative to the well-
being of the self is inevitably involved. Freud (1920) himself noted
that anxiety in the form of signal anxiety served adaptive purposes
through an evaluation of relative safety. Emde (1989) has noted
that beginning at about 12 or 13 months exploring children will
look to the caretaker to see whether or not their actions are safe, a
behavior Emde calls "social referencing."

Social referencing, then, probably serves as the basis for the
child's learning to take inner experiences as indicators of the well-
being of the self relative to the situations encountered in the external world. Social referencing, however, also occurs in relation to
the caretaker's evaluation of the child's behavior or performance.
Thus, the meaning of inner experiences also serves as an evaluator
of the relative goodness or badness of the individual. Meaning thus
serves as an indicator of self-evaluation or self-esteem.

Participation in a Human Community

Meaning also involves Sullivan's (1953) concept of consensual validation, which can be understood as a truth discovered through
sharing with others. Sullivan believed that consensual validation,
which takes place particularly within preadolescent same-sex relationships, leads the individual to develop a new sense of humanity
through belonging to a human community. Seton (1981) has similarly noted that human beings like to experience strong emotions
because they make us feel human.

Although psychoanalysts have recently been paying more attention to the sense of self-esteem that can be achieved from effectance (White, 1963) or competence (Basch, 1988), the sense of self-
confirmation, satisfaction, and/or fulfillment that comes from
feeling that one has participated fully within a human community
has received little attention. It is, nevertheless, a fundamental and
important aspect of human life. Human beings are indeed social
animals, and Erikson (1963) was certainly correct in maintaining

that a sense of identity is not possible without a sense of belonging to some group.

In summary, meaning can be seen to have at least four distinguishable but interrelated functions: (1) communication, (2) organization, (3) evaluation, and (4) confirmation of the self as a participant in a human community. Each of these functions has both interpersonal and intrapsychic aspects. Meaning, therefore, provides a conceptually needed bridge between the interpersonal and the intrapsychic.

3 Identity and the Self

Erikson's (1963, 1980) work has always been popular with social workers, largely because of his attempt to place Freud's psychosexual stages of development in a social context. His concept of identity has also been heavily utilized. Clinically, for example, clients are thought to need a sense of their own relationship to social and historical forces, as well as a sense of the meaning of this position for themselves as well as for others. It has always been considered unhealthy to deny some aspect of personal identity, whether that be sexual, racial, ethnic, religious, or some other dimension.

One of the functions of the concept of identity, then, has been to connect the individual to the social environment. Theoretically, the nature of such a connection would depend on underlying assumptions about the nature of external reality. As has already been indicated, Freud adhered to the notion that reality is knowable through observation, and this assumption is implicit in Erikson's work as well. This perspective leads to the belief that the healthiest persons are those whose identity is "in touch with reality," that is, those whose understanding of themselves is the most consonant with the true features of the external world and of their relationship to that world.

Since, from this point of view, there is one correct picture of reality, then there must also be one correct identity. Erikson does not, of course, specify that there is one correct identity. However, he places considerable emphasis on the fact that the consolidation of identity is a normal occurrence in adolescence. The alternative to identity consolidation is identity diffusion, which is pathologic. Erikson describes in considerable detail the many difficulties encountered if the normal process of consolidation does not occur. Thus, Erikson appears to adopt a unitary concept of identity. This, of course, also fits with Freud's view that intrapsychic conflict leads to pathology. A major problem with this approach is that if there is one correct picture of reality, then there must also be one picture of what is normal or healthy. Social workers have known for years that a static picture of health is not workable and that normal or healthy behavior cannot be defined in the absence of considerations about varying contexts of behavior.

If it is assumed that an understanding of reality is constructed, then there are many lenses through which to look at the external world and the pictures of reality yielded by each lens, though still reasonable reflections of selected aspects of the world, will differ. If reality is constructed, then having a unitary identity will not, in fact, be adaptive. Instead, in order for the individual to be able to comprehend the possibility of a range of choices, he or she will need to have a multifaceted identity. Furthermore, there will necessarily be a number of behavioral patterns, all of which would be considered normal or healthy.

Erikson (1980, p. 158) noted that there were similarities between his concept of identity and the "self" of the sociologist George Herbert Mead. Mead (1934) conceived of the self as developing out of social interactions; that is, the characteristics of the self were acquired not only from parents, as in the oedipal stage of traditional psychoanalytic theory, but from any and all social interactions in which the person participated. The result was, of course, a much more complex and richly imagined self. Although Mead indicated that there was an organizing or generalizing factor involved, the self was not considered to be unitary. There were as many selves as there were social roles.

> We carry on a whole series of different relationships to different people. We are one thing to one man and another thing to another. There are parts of the self which exist only for the self in relationship to itself. We divide ourselves up in all sorts of different selves with reference to our acquaintances. We discuss politics with one and religion with another. There are all sorts of different selves answering to all sorts of different social reactions. (Mead, 1934, p. 142)

The need for a concept of identity complexity is not yet generally recognized. However, recently there have been a few clinical theorists who have commented on it. Guidano (1987) has written the following:

The perception of a many-sided self is indeed a pervasive and crucial issue of our experiencing life. Each one of us not only has different perceptions and evaluations of ourself in relation to different domains of experience—work, private life, social life, and so on—but also, within each domain, experience changes in the sense of self according to the quality and intensity of the ongoing emotional experiences. Each of these self-images, in turn, is simultaneously experienced both in the present and in the anticipated future, for example, the potential or "ideal" self-images.

Personal identity, therefore, rather than being a defined entity or a superordinate concept, is like an ongoing process whose recursive nature gives functional unity and historical continuity to the individual coalition of self-subsystems. Due to this integrative capacity, the individual, at any moment and according to particular environmental influences, has a perceived identity that represents merely a single example of his/her range of possible self-images. Furthermore, each self-representation is always perceived as a global experience. This is because conscious focal attention selectively amplifies the working self-structures, while at the same time, inhibits others from rising to active awareness. (pp. 85–86)

The idea of a complex experience of the self is often implied but not directly stated by more psychodynamically oriented writers. Mitchell (1988, p. 265), for example, indicated that individuals who have been analyzed end up experiencing themselves as multitextured and uneven, with a sense of a more complex life. The idea that the ability to experience complexity is a fundamental aspect of health is also implied in the work of Mahler and her followers (Blanck & Blanck, 1974; Mahler et al., 1975), who see the capacity to tolerate ambivalence as a primary indicator of object constancy.

Searles (1979), while not emphasizing this point in a theoretical overview, directly states the following:

Perhaps due in part to a too-literal interpretation of some of Erikson's early writings concerning ego identity, I long thought the sense of identity in a healthy individual to be essentially monolithic in nature, consisting in large part of well-digested part-identifications with other persons. . . . But in more recent years, especially in the course of my exploring the psychodynamics of the borderline patient, in whom the sense of identity coexists simultaneously in two or more internal objects, I have come to see that the healthy individual's sense of identity is far from being monolithic in nature. It involves, rather, myriad internal objects functioning in lively and harmonious interrelatedness, and all contributing to a relatively coherent, consistent sense of identity which springs from and comprises all of them, but does not involve their being congealed into any so unitary a mass as I once thought. I have come to believe that the more healthy an individual is, the more consciously does he live in the knowledge that there are myriad "persons"—internal objects each bearing some sense-of-identity value—within him; and he recognizes this state of his internal world to be what it is; not threatened insanity, but the strength resident in the human condition. (p. 462)

Mead's idea of multiple selves has been very popular in sociology and social psychology, where identity has been related to reference groups. Identity is considered the result of the individual's attempts to locate himself or herself in the system of social roles through asking the question "Who am I?" (Sarbin & Scheibe, 1983). Although the notion of identity as related to the individual's validated social positions is a logical conceptualization, sociology has had more difficulty, until recently, in being able to explicate satisfactorily the details of the process of socialization through which the person comes to take on this identity.

Although Mead saw the self as arising in social interaction, he, as a behaviorist, did not see meaning as an intrapsychic phenomenon. For him, the meaning of an action was defined by the response of the other person to that action. This definition does not allow for any conception of independent intention on the part of the individual. Furthermore, Mead saw the individual essentially as a smaller version of the social system. For Mead (1934, p. 144), the organization of any self was identical with the organization of the social group within which that person was engaged. Thus, although in a different sense than is true of psychoanalytic theory, Mead also assumed a rather static relationship between the individual and the external world.

Unfortunately, there has been a tendency, particularly in some academic and research circles, in social work to assume that Mead's equation would actually hold, even though it has not generally been held up to serious scrutiny. Thus, it has frequently been expected that the results of certain types of demographic or symptom surveys, as well as epidemiologic research, would have direct meaning for how to conduct clinical work with individuals, families, and small groups. Clinicians, of course, know that while data regarding how a large number of people experience something is interesting, only Mrs. Jones knows if she shares in that experience. For the clinician to assume that she either does or should is to stereotype her. The self of the individual and its organization cannot be equated with the social process or with the organization of the group. The individual is both more and less than the collective.

Currently, some social psychologists have adopted the idea that the self is constituted in social discourse (Shotter, 1989). Within such a conceptualization the identity of the self still has a social origin; furthermore, the meaning content of the identity can be seen as constituted within the interaction between the knower, the known, and a sharer. Such a conceptualization does not so readily lend itself to the creation of stereotypes, since the meaning content of the individual's identity would largely depend upon the particular interactions in which that individual had been engaged.

Definitions

As can be seen from the preceding paragraphs, there is considerable confusion and overlap in the definitions of the concepts of the self and identity. The current popularity of self psychology and the accompanying move away from drive theory have resulted in an increased focus on the concept of the self. There have been a variety of definitions of self, but little attention has been given to the manner in which a concept of self might relate to the concept of identity.

Erikson (1980) explained his concept of identity as follows:

> At one time, then, it will appear to refer to a conscious *sense of individual identity*; at another to an unconscious striving for a *continuity of personal character*; at a third, as a criterion for the silent doings of *ego synthesis*; and, finally, as a maintenance of an inner *solidarity with a group's ideals and identity.* (p. 109)

Erikson has been criticized for including a number of ideas and functions in his identity concept, a practice that has resulted in a lack of conceptual clarity (see, for example, Lichtenstein, 1977). Certainly Erikson's identity concept has had an enormous appeal, but it is possible that some of this appeal is due to the fact that the concept is too global to be broken down for use in specific and analytic contexts.

However, the same criticism can be made of some definitions of the self. Basch (1983), for example, provided the following definition:

> The self is not a thing or an entity; it is a concept: a symbolic abstraction from the developmental process. The self refers to the

uniqueness that separates the experiences of an individual from those of all others while at the same time conferring a sense of cohesion and continuity on the disparate experiences of that individual throughout his life. The self is the symbolic transformation of experience into an overall goal-directed construct. (p. 53)

Clinical theory would be improved by definitions of self and identity that distinguish these ideas from each other and that can be couched in somewhat less confusing terms.

"Self is process; life is motion," according to Sanville (1987, p. 265). However, she also says, "That which we call self is closely identified with the meaning schemes at which we have arrived at any particular point in time" (p. 264). She further points out that the concept of the self must do double duty as both an experiential entity and a regulatory agency. In culling out the aspects of process and of meaning schemes or systems, Sanville has identified two critical elements that have been basic to the concepts of self and identity as they have variously been used.

In this book self is being defined as the process involved in experiencing or creating meaning. The processes of the self develop with the experience and maturation of the individual and underlie the capacity to create meaning. The self is fundamentally social; although the processes involved have biological bases, their function is to guide interactive exchanges with other human beings so that meaning is created. In the absence of interactive exchanges with other human beings, particularly in the early years of life, these processes are likely to remain underdeveloped or to deteriorate. The processes of the self can be studied within a scientific, causal mode of thinking.

Identity is composed of the content of the meaningful experiences of the individual, whether these have been formally constructed into conscious meaning systems or remain more at the level of sensations that can potentially be converted into conscious meaning systems. Since meaning systems can only be created through an interactive social process, identity is also a social phenomenon. Identity can be studied in the mode of thinking identified by Bruner as the "narrative construction of the possible" but does not fit well into the framework of causal science.

One of the important functions of the concepts of self and identity, noted by both Basch and Erikson, is the provision of a sense of continuity or selfsameness. Clinical evidence has established beyond much question the fact that human beings need a sense of organization and of continuity in time in order to be able to function adequately. This evidence has undoubtedly been a major factor in influencing theorists to conceptualize the healthy personality as one that is stable—almost to the point of being static—following the developmental years from infancy through adolescence.

The previous failure to separate out the capacity to create meaning from the content of the meaning created, however, has contributed to formulations of a static identity. Erikson, for example, referred to identity as insuring the continuity of one's meaning for others in the society. However, it is simply inaccurate to assume that any individual has the same meaning to all members of any social group at any one time. Furthermore, any individual's meaning, to himself or herself or to others, is a constantly changing thing. Meaning must always be related to the context of the moment, and since experience and the environment are constantly changing, meaning systems must be continually updated and actively maintained. Identity, as the individual's meaning system, is therefore constantly changing.

How then can the individual's experience of continuity be explained? From an objective perspective, the experience of self-sameness can only be seen as an illusion. From a subjective point of view, it would appear that the sense of continuity is provided by the stories people create about their lives that constitute the meaning systems of identity. Narrative is the form in which human beings organize their experience. In that sense it is narrative that is the result of the process that has been called the "synthetic function of the ego" (Schafer, 1980). Since narrative organizes events along temporal lines within which there are causal connections, the stories that individuals construct about themselves provide them with a sense of organization that relates not just to the present but to the past and the future as well. The organized content of an individual's identity or meaning system is therefore important to functioning and to a sense of well-being.

The activity involved in the process of the creation of meaning, what is being defined here as the self, probably also contributes to a sense of continuity. The capacity to create meaning, which is the result of the activity of the self, normally develops over time, especially in the early years of life. There can be shifts in the processes underlying this capacity at any time in life, and these may result in either an improvement or a decrease in functioning. When major shifts in the processes of the self occur the individual probably experiences disruption in the sense of continuity. Under most circumstances, however, these changes occur much more slowly than do shifts in the content of the identity meaning system.

It is now possible to note that the improvements that occur in treatment may result from either a shift in the content of identity or from an increase in the capacity to create meaning. In some instances it may be possible to achieve a significant change in a client's identity and thereby increase social functioning in a relatively short time. However, since rapidly occurring major changes in the meaning systems of identity threaten the individual's sense of organization and continuity, lasting major content changes normally come about more slowly. Many clients, however, have difficulty in creating meaning of any sort and require help in developing the capacity to do so. Increasing the client's capacity to create meaning seems to be what psychoanalytic theorists have referred to as "structural change" and usually requires long-term therapy.

In treatment, as in the actual functioning of any individual, the processes of the self are constantly creating the content of the meaning systems of identity. The processes of the self and the meaning systems of identity are therefore intimately interrelated and are separable only conceptually. As a result, although some treatment strategies may involve greater shifts in either the processes of the self or the meaning systems of identity, successes in most treatment enterprises must be seen as being due to changes in both self and identity.

Psychological Health

In spite of the fact that clinicians have been engaged in helping others improve their mental health for many years, it has been difficult to define just what mental health actually is. Freud's statement that mental health is the ability to love and to work is often quoted and, indeed, remains a reasonable statement. It does not, however, lead to a specification of what qualities, characteristics, or experiences enable a human being to function well.

In addition, Freud's work implied at least three different criteria for mental health, all of which involve serious problems. First, the belief in the importance of the Oedipus complex and its resolution not only overvalues the place of genital functioning in human life but is fundamentally sexist. Second, the idea that human beings need to be free of the distortions in reality perception caused by affects and need states in order to achieve a desirable rationality relies on faulty assumptions about both the accuracy of observation and the interrelationships between cognition and affect. Finally, the equation of intrapsychic conflict with pathology fails to recognize that some ambivalence and inner conflict is healthy and that some severely pathologic states involve little conflict but also little inner experience (Saari, 1986).

Were it possible to specify certain behaviors that are healthy and others that are not, the problem of defining psychological health would undoubtedly have been solved easily. But behavior that is appropriate and healthy in one situation is not in another. Even the same sexual behavior that Freud saw as serving an exemplary function may be indicative of a healthy intimacy in one situation and of a frantic attempt to avert fragmentation in another. Since judgments about the appropriateness of behavior must be determined on the basis of the particular situation under consideration, it is conceivable that there might be a one-to-one correspondence between a situation and the appropriate behavior. This solution, however, has failed in the sense that it relies on a system in which there is only one possible accurate perception and one truth.

Recently, theories of mental health have frequently utilized a developmental viewpoint. Currently, however, there are a number of controversies over the usefulness of a developmental point of view. Werner (1978) rightly indicates that the concept of development always involves directionality. In other words, it is not possible to talk about development unless one is prepared to answer the question, Development toward what? One of the criticisms of the developmental concept, then, involves its reliance on a value judgment. The whole idea of directionality means that there are higher and lower forms of the phenomenon in question. The pure, empirical (logical positivist) view of science held that true knowledge is based on objective observations and that value judgments had no place in science. A current constructivist point of view, however, argues that *all* theories involve judgments; from this perspective, no theory is ever value-free. The idea of a value-free science has always been an impossible one for social work as a discipline. Value judgments, such as the conviction that all human beings have an inherent dignity and that all should have equal opportunities and justice, constitute the very essence of a professional social work perspective (Imre, 1982). Without the professional value system, social work, as understood by its early founders, simply cannot exist. The issue then becomes not one of trying to get rid of the value judgments but, rather, of creating a theory compatible with social work's value system.

The specification of the ideal state toward which the healthy individual develops has, of course, been a difficult issue. Freud's notion of genital primacy, as has already been indicated, was quite inadequate. Mahler's (Mahler et al., 1975) idea of separation–individuation has frequently been criticized as being essentially located in an individualistically oriented value system that is fundamentally alien to social work. Hartmann's (1958) idea of pleasure in functioning is more consonant with social work values. The idea that each individual should have the opportunity to develop his or her capacities to the fullest extent possible has been fundamental to social work. This point of view can be combined with the idea that the creation of meaning is fundamental and essential to what gives human beings their humanness. The ideal end point for mental health then becomes the greatest possible development of the individual's capacity to create meaning.

Mental health, then, involves the greatest possible development of the processes of the self. It should be pointed out here that in some individuals there may be inherent limitations on the extent to which the capacity to create meaning can develop. Such limitations may be genetically or physiologically determined. Psychological health, however, would be the greatest possible utilization of whatever potential is inherent in any given person. For this reason, health would need to be determined on an individual basis. Furthermore, it should be assumed that human beings are never able to utilize their potential fully and that is not possible to evaluate totally just what the full potential of any individual might be. Thus, some relativity will always be involved in judgments regarding psychological health.

There have also been a number of criticisms of developmental theory's notion of linear causation and its simplistic attempt to account for human functioning. Such criticisms are undoubtedly warranted in relation to the epigenetic form that most developmental theories to date have taken (e.g., Freud, Piaget, Mahler, Erikson,). It is becoming clear that the notion of epigenetic stages is not the only format in which development can be understood. Stern (1985), for example, has utilized the idea of domains that are crystallized at certain ages but that then coexist with each other for the remainder of the person's life. Stern's theory therefore has the ability to account for much more complexity in the functioning of the human being. It is likely that developmental concepts other than domains and epigenetic stages may be conceived in the future and may further improve the ability of our theories to capture the richness of human functioning.

Although Erikson has been criticized for utilizing an epigenetic framework (Lichtenstein, 1977), he did extend his stages throughout the human being's life cycle. It is important to understand that meaning cannot simply be created once, with the expectation that it will then remain forever unchanged. Meaning systems must be constantly maintained and amended. Therefore, the functioning of the self must be an active process throughout life. It is clear that these processes can change, resulting in either an increasing or decreasing ability, at any time in life. From the perspective used here, the specific content of Erikson's stages in the life cycle may be open to question. However, it is apparent from Erikson's conceptualization of the stages in the later part of the life cycle that he did have the important underlying assumption that the healthy individual continues to create meaning until death.

Is psychological health related to the content of the meaning created by the processes of the self? Is it possible to make a judgment about relative mental health based on the content of the identity system? It should already be clear that no one construction of the world can be considered to capture truth. However, since identity is a meaning system, standards used to judge the adequacy of meaning systems can be applied here. The central criterion is the relative coherence of the identity systems. It is important to stress that the concepts of a lack of coherence and a lack of conflict are not the same. It is possible to express or to experience a conflict in a clear and coherent way that would not here be considered to be in the least pathologic. Thus, conflict may well exist in a healthy, coherent meaning system. There undoubtedly is a limit to the amount of conflict that a person can experience at any given time and retain a sense of coherence, but it is the degree of retained coherence, not the existence of conflict per se, that is the critical element on which psychological health can be judged.

In the object relations literature, especially in the writings of Kernberg (1975) and other followers of Melanie Klein (1952), much has been made of the phenomenon of defensive splitting as an indication of primitive functioning. Klein based her conception of splitting on the idea that the child, in order to tolerate powerfully experienced ambivalence toward the caretaking object early in life, must keep good and bad objects rigidly defined and separated. Such a formulation may rely too heavily on specifications of intensity in the early affective experience of the child, but the tendency to evaluate experience in terms of whether it is good or bad does seem to be an inborn tendency of the human infant (Lewis & Brooks-Gunn, 1979; Stern, 1985). Certainly it is true that a meaning system in which things are divided only into rigidly held polar opposites will not be effective in being able to contain conflict and retain coherence. Moreover, the splitting often seen in low-functioning clients may be indicative not merely of strongly experienced ambivalence toward caretakers but of a generalized inability to comprehend more than two possibilities in any situation.

Schafer (1976) has stressed the importance for psychological health of accepting responsibility for one's own actions. However, this has sometimes been considered to be a punitive attitude toward clients. One of the problems with Freud's failure to distinguish between motivation, meaning, and causation is a tendency to assume that the result of any action must be what the individual unconsciously desired. Yet the environment has an existence independent of the individual, and people cannot always control or even foresee the results of their actions. From this perspective, then, Schafer's expectation of accepting responsibility for one's own actions seems punitive.

On the other hand, if it is understood that the person must accept responsibility for the choice of action rather than for the actual result of the action, the statement no longer seems unnecessarily punitive. Defining psychological health as a capacity to create meaning indicates that it is important for people to know that choices for behavior exist and that they must take responsibility for considering the predictable consequences of the alternatives. Similarly, the individual may have to take responsibility for having made a choice that turned out to be unfortunate, but this should not be equated either with the person's having in some unconscious manner wished for the result or necessarily being responsible for the result. Insisting that people understand the existence of choice encourages a stance toward the world as "objects of contemplation" rather than as "things-of-action", a stance from which meaning can be created (Werner & Kaplan, 1963).

The more possibilities the individual can envision in any given situation, the more alternatives that person can consider in the selection of behavior. Thus, the possibility of adaptive behavior is increased by a multifaceted comprehension of the world. The systems theorists von Bertalanffy (1968) and Werner (1978) see systems as developing in the direction of increasing articulation, differentiation, and integration. It is possible, therefore, to see the meaning systems of identity as developing in the direction of increasing articulation, differentiation and integration. It would, then, be the quality of this complexity that would indicate psychological health rather than the specific content of the meaning systems created.

This is further to suggest that self-knowledge is not, as is commonly assumed, the product of in-depth probing of the inner recesses of the psyche. It is not the result of active sensitivity to the nuances of emotion, motivation, intention and the like. Rather, it is a mastery of discourse—a "knowing how" rather than a "knowing that." This is not at all to subtract from the importance of such discourse. Rather, without grasping the linguistic skills to make the inner world come to life, one ceases to become a full participant—with all the rights that may accrue—in social life. Thus it is not the person who professes a flagging self-esteem, a low level of morale or a guilty conscience who has an "inadequate" conception of self: each of these forms of self-accounting can be vitally effective, and often enable one to achieve a certain form of power in social life. Rather, it is the inarticulate or linguistically undifferentiated individual who requires attention. Such an individual is simply bereft of the symbolic resources necessary for full social functioning. (Gergen, 1989, pp. 75–76)

In other words, the person who has a differentiated and articulated inner life may have difficulty with experienced conflict either with the inner or the external world but is also in a position to be able to make decisions regarding how to deal with that conflict. Conflict in human life seems to be ubiquitous and unavoidable; the individual who does not have an articulated and integrated inner life does not have the resources to deal with it.

Psychological health can, therefore, be defined as a highly developed capacity to create meaning, with the result of that capacity being identity complexity.

4 Culture as a Shared Meaning System

Psychological health has been defined in this book as a highly developed capacity to create meaning, with the result of that capacity being identity complexity. This definition of mental health is a departure from the concept of adaptation, the more traditional approach in social work as well as in other mental health disciplines. Certainly, the idea of mental illness as the result of a failure to adapt is a more humanitarian notion than earlier ideas of mental illness as evidence of sinfulness or the influence of the devil. However, viewing health as properly adapted behavior has also created some serious problems for clinical social workers.

Advocates of an adaptational point of view have wished to see mental health as the outcome of an interaction between the person and the environment, but the bulk of clinical work takes place directly with the client rather than with the environment. To some, a preference for this viewpoint implies a judgment by the clinician that the "failure" to adapt is on the client's part, betraying an attitude of "blaming the victim." In the 1960s many social workers began to criticize casework as simply a means of adapting people to a sick society that offered neither equality nor justice. Other clinicians, having noticed that interventions that change only the environment often do not result in the elimination of problems related to individual functioning, were apt to think of treatment involving only environmental intervention as being unsophisticated and ineffective.

These observations continue to contribute to some tension between policy advocates who wish to intervene in society and clinicians whose skill is in work with individuals, families, and small

groups. This tension persists even though these professionals espouse essentially the same goals and values; it has continued
largely because the problem is located within practice rather than
within the theoretical framework in which it is understood.

There have been other problems in the adaptational perspective
for the clinician as well. This perspective contains the implication
that the healthy individual is "in touch with reality" and that therefore there is some achievable accurate perception of the truth
about the world. An effective clinician would then, presumably,
need to have a view of the world that is superior to the client's,
implying a somewhat authoritarian client–social worker relationship. However, this contradicts practice wisdom that indicates that
treatment is more effective when the client–social worker relationship is collaborative rather than authoritarian. Furthermore, while
experience has indicated that advice and information giving may
sometimes be useful, these are not the major tools of the clinician
(Woods and Hollis, 1990).

Uncoupling psychological health from adaptation has several
beneficial results. It removes the punitive implication that failure
to achieve according to society's standards means an individual
must not be sufficiently healthy. It removes the burden from the
clinician of having to be omniscient and allows for a more collaborative treatment relationship. It also means there need not be sur-
prise at the fact that the biographies of socially designated heroes
or heroines frequently indicate considerable psychological pathology. Furthermore, it means that achieving a state of psychological
health through treatment does not guarantee that the client's behavior will be consonant with the current prescriptions of the
existing social order. Instead, it means that the client will take such
prescriptions, as well as the probable consequences of the behavior, into consideration in making behavioral choices.

Uncoupling psychological health from adaptation, then, has
some advantages for clinical social work theory. However, social
work has always understood the uniqueness of its own perspective
on the world, when contrasted to that of other mental health
professions, as involving a person–environment interaction. Does
uncoupling psychological health from adaptation mean that the
clinician can ignore environmental considerations? The answer to
this question is a resounding no, but some shifts in the theoretical
framework explaining the function of these considerations of environmental conditions need to be made. A brief return to the
theory behind an adaptational point of view will help to begin an

exploration of the relevance of a person–environment perspective for clinical work.

The concept of adaptation in the sense of an organism whose characteristics and behavior especially equip it to survive in its environment derives, of course, from Darwin's work on evolution, which preceded Freud's work by only a few decades. The theory of evolution had a major impact on the 19th-century scientific climate within which Freud and his followers developed their ideas. Although Freud enthusiastically endorsed Darwinian theory (Gay, 1988), he did not devote much attention to issues relating to the environment, essentially because of his belief that human cognition produced an accurate picture of the world. He expected that psychoanalysis would contribute significantly to the elimination of the irrational distortions, caused by emotions and need states, of this reality. Thus, psychological health or properly adapted rational behavior could be fostered in human beings without having to consider the nature of the environment. Once humans had access to the" true" picture of the world, as guaranteed by perception, they would automatically be able to behave in ways that were attuned to the environment.

While Freud took for granted that the psychologically healthy individual would also be adapted to the environment, Hartmann (1958) introduced a consideration of the concept of adaptation into psychoanalysis and espoused the idea of adaptation as a therapeutic aim. He pointed out that it is not possible to think of adaptation without considering the nature of the environment, without asking the question Adaptation to what? In addition, his theory paid much more attention to the interaction between an individual and the environment than had Freud, and it introduced the idea that an adaptive balance could be achieved through changes in the individual or in the environment or in seeking a totally new environment for the individual.

In spite of this sophisticated theorizing, Hartmann accepted a more or less direct relationship between psychological health and adaptation. Since mental health ought to vary in differing environments, he proposed that judging individual health in clinical work required the assumption of a constant or "average expectable environment." Here Hartmann's theory becomes problematic, because a definition of an average expectable environment, expressed in other than highly ethnocentric terms, is difficult to conceive. Certainly, the notion of an environment that remains constant violates everyday experience. Assuming a constant environment basically undermined Hartmann's more interactive intent, but it allowed for the continuation of psychoanalytic practice as Freud had described it; that is, psychoanalytic practice had always dealt with the patient's meaning system and had not presumed the need to collect data about the existing environment.

The idea of symptomatology as the result of failed efforts to adapt to the environment has had a major influence on American conceptions of mental illness, not only through the direct influence of Hartmann's ideas but also through the work of Adolph Meyer (1957). Meyer, who was also strongly influenced by Darwin, was one of the earliest teachers of psychiatry in this country. In contrast to Hartmann's more intrapsychically based views, Meyer's interest was in the specific influences of the environment. He believed that mental illness was the result of the individual's attempts to adapt to a too rapidly changing environment. Meyer's students have been influential in both epidemiology and the community mental health movement.

The idea that an environment that was changing too rapidly or was unsupportive contributed to mental illness was certainly a part of the thinking of the early social workers. Mary Richmond (1917), for example, advocated that workers collect extensive data on the client's environment, including information from interviewing neighbors, employers, and coworkers. Although under some circumstances specific knowledge of the client's environment is considered important, current practice does not include this kind of data gathering, which would now be considered demeaning to the client and a violation of the right to confidentiality.

Clinical social workers have, of course, long known that it is important to work with the client's understanding of his or her environment, and this tenet has normally dictated the techniques of practice. In spite of this recognition in regard to practice, however, it has not always been appreciated that a person's relationship to the environment simply cannot be understood in the absence of considerations about the intervening variable of the meaning system through which the person understands the environment. This is not simply a guideline for clinical practice; it is a required element in any theory regarding human behavior.

In spite of the problems in Hartmann's supposition of an average expectable environment, some of his considerations regarding adaptation are consonant with an understanding of the importance of meaning systems and have some real advantages. Hartmann did not consider humans to be merely passive in the adaptive process but thought of them as actively involved in relating to the environment. He believed that the organism derives a sense of pleasure from the very exercise of its functions and that there is an inborn push toward health in human beings that makes it possible to conceive of symptomatology as the result of abortive attempts at healthy adaptation. The adaptational point of view, then, has had some usefulness as well as limitations.

Freud has frequently been criticized for his neglect of considerations relative to culture. Hartmann, although more aware of the element of culture, failed to make a sufficient distinction between culture and society. For example, in discussing his concept of adaptation, Hartmann (1958) says, "It may not be superfluous to mention again that by adaptation we do not mean only passive submission to the goals of society, but also active collaboration on them and attempts to change them" (p. 32). In this passage Hartmann speaks not of the individual's relationship to the society as an organizational structure external to the individual but, rather, to its goals. Goals, however, can be distinguished from the social organization and seen, instead, to be a part of the culture. The importance of a difference between culture as a meaning system and social structure has only recently become apparent.

Under the umbrella of a 19th-century model of science, in which knowledge was derived purely from observation of the world, culture was thought to be logically derived from the existing reality of the environment, both social and physical. However, as a constructivist worldview has become more common, the conception of culture has also been changing:

> It would not be an exaggeration to say that in the last decade there has been a revolution in the definition of human culture. It takes the form of a move away from the strict structuralism that held that culture was a set of interconnected rules from which people derive particular behaviors to fit particular situations, to the idea of culture as implicit and only semiconnected knowledge of the world from which, through negotiation, people arrive at satisfactory ways of acting in given contexts. (Bruner, 1986, p. 65)

Becker (1986) has defined culture as the shared understandings that people use to coordinate their activities. Culture, then, can be understood as a shared meaning system.

If culture is conceived of as a shared meaning system, then it would seem consistent with Hartmann's meaning of adaptation to think of mental health as the ability to participate in the cultural meaning system. In saying that mental health is dependent on the individual having "an integrated universe consistent within the given cultural framework," von Bertalanffy (1968, p. 219) has indicated a similar conception; through participation in a shared meaning system the individual would achieve a meaningful sense of participation in the human community. It is important, however, to agree with Hartmann that such participation does not merely mean compliance with set precepts but, rather, "active collaboration and attempts to change them."

Psychological health, then, makes it possible for people to understand and participate in the cultural meaning system around them. This does not guarantee that the individual will make choices that will be in compliance with the dictates within the social system, especially since it would be within the realm of possibility for the healthy person to decide that the social system was not fair and to choose to protest or defy it. The person who could not understand or participate in the cultural meaning system would not have a range of choices for behavior and would be much less likely to be able to choose to defy the society in an organized and meaningful manner. Psychological health does, however, enable social functioning in that the healthy person has a sense of how he or she relates to the cultural meaning system and can make behavioral choices on the basis of this knowledge.

In other words, it is the development of the capacity to create meaning that makes it possible for the individual to comprehend and participate in the culture, thereby permitting effective social functioning. A clinical judgment about the relative development of this capacity in any given individual can usually be made on the basis of coherence criteria without knowledge of the specifics of the client's particular environment. The clinical judgment would be based on (1) the relative differentiation, articulation, and coherence of identity content and (2) the relative ability to participate in human interaction for purposes of the creation of meaning. Such a judgment does not, however, provide the clinician with any reliable information as to the specific cause of any deficiencies found within that capacity.

Too often in the past, clinical theories have suggested the idea of isolating "the cause" of the client's problem and then addressing that cause. Multiple cause is the rule rather than the exception. Clinicians need to be aware of the possibility of causal factors related to inborn biological factors, to insufficient or distorted interpersonal interactions within the immediate environment, and to conditions within the broader physical environment or society. In some instances, the clinician will need to call upon other professionals, such as physicians, to help address problems related to these causal factors.

Since human beings must define their identity, the ability to participate in the meaning systems of the social groups of which they are a part is important to the maintenance of mental health. Structures at any level of society that deny access to participation, in the sense of the ability to play a part in the determination of the content of the culture, significantly diminish the likelihood of the achievement or maintenance of a capacity to create meaning in those individuals to whom such access is denied. Other environmental conditions, such as an inadequacy in health care, employment opportunities, nutrition, and housing, can also limit the individual's capacity to function at maximum potential. Thus, the clinician may need to intervene within the environment in order to insure to the client an environment within which a capacity to create meaning can be exercised.

In cases in which there is a capacity to create meaning that has been insufficiently developed to allow for the degree of effective social functioning desired by the client and in which the current environment is capable of tolerating the exercise of such a capacity, treatment in the form of adjustments in the content of meaning systems and/or practicing the capacity to create meaning in order to refine it is indicated. This treatment is indicated regardless of what the original cause of the deficit may have been. It is this treatment to which the clinical social worker normally devotes the bulk of his or her time and attention.

From this perspective it becomes clear that the clinical social worker needs to know about both culture and the environment. The judgments that clinical social workers are regularly called upon to make in planning and carrying out intervention into either the client or the environment can be seen to be multifaceted and to require knowledge about both the client's ability to participate in culture and the social environment's ability to permit and support that functioning. The clinical social worker needs to be able to utilize in an integrated fashion knowledge from the realm of meaning as well as from the realm of causal science. It is no wonder that clinical social work is such a demanding profession.

Culture and Thought

Participation in the culture does not require one to subscribe to the ideas and practices dominant in the culture, but it does require an acquaintance with them. Although interpersonal transactions occur throughout the life cycle, the most concentrated period of learning cultural meaning systems occurs during early childhood. There is a wealth of sociological and anthropological literature on the manner in which child-rearing practices acquaint the next generation with the culture and prepare it for life within the presumably expectable conditions of the social and physical environment. Culture is conveyed through a number of activities, with the use of language having a prominent involvement in these.

In recent years the idea that culture determines thought through the medium of language has received considerable attention. A linguist named Whorf (1971) noticed that Eskimos have numerous words for various types of snow whereas English has only one word for this substance. He then proposed that the availability of words in a language determines thought. It has since been noted that a lack of specific words to distinguish qualities of objects in the concrete physical surround does not always prevent perception; English speakers, for example, do note differences between powdery and slushy snow in spite of not having separate words for these substances (Bruner, Olver & Greenfield, 1966).

Language does not, however, confine itself simply to common nouns for concrete objects that are observable within the environment. Language provides its speakers with an entire set of concepts, often hierarchically arranged, that indicate how the observables in the environment are related to each other. Many of these everyday concepts have no referent in observable reality. One cannot, for example, observe a "furniture," a concept grouping together on the basis of generalized usage a class of objects of quite different qualities in relation to size, appearance, and composition.

The ability to utilize a categorical system in which the category criteria are consistently maintained has been considered to be basic to adequate psychological functioning. For example, if one wished to categorize a number of red, white, and blue pencils on the basis of color, it would be inappropriate to add to the blue grouping a brown pencil that happened to be the same length as the blue pencils. This categorizing principle was the basis for the object sorting test on which Singer (1965) demonstrated that parents of schizophrenic patients had considerable difficulty. This finding has been used as a basis for the view that the inability of such parents to teach the proper utilization of categories contributed to the mental illness of their offspring.

Although consistency is required in the appropriate utilization of a categorical system, any object can appropriately be placed within a number of categories, depending on the aspect judged to be of significance for the purpose at hand. For example, a desk would belong to the categories of furniture, objects made of wood, objects with flat surface for writing, and so forth. While language does not fully determine perception, the aspects of any given object for which there are commonly used categorical systems within a culture are more apt to be noticed. Furthermore, since the categories themselves are linked to each other in conceptual systems that delineate cause and effect and explain the world, thought is determined by language in that it is dependent upon the categories and conceptual systems that language makes available.

While a strict empiricist approach to the world assumed that the categories of thought were derived directly from the external world, this is no longer considered to be the case. Von Bertalanffy (1968) has pointed out that the survival of a culture requires that its concepts be isomorphic with the conditions of the environment but not that they be identical. Thus, adaptation to the physical environment in the Darwinian sense of survival can occur in the absence of a possessed "truth."

Individuals are not likely to think of a relationship or explanation for which there is no preexisting category or concept available within their culture. In recent years, for example, feminists have argued that so long as there were concepts and categories related to castrating women but not to chauvinistic men, women were likely to be less conscious of their social oppression. Homosexual social constructivists such as Tiefer (1987) have pointed out that the existence of only two genders is a matter of arbitrary cultural agreement.

Von Bertalanffy (1968) noted the reciprocity between language and culture:

> It may be mentioned, in passing, that the relation between language and world view is not unidirectional but reciprocal, a fact which perhaps was not made sufficiently clear by Whorf. The structure of language seems to determine which traits of reality are abstracted and hence what form the categories of thinking take on. On the other hand, the world outlook determines and forms the language. (p. 238)

This reciprocity undoubtedly accounts for the fact that most thought tends to remain within the limits of the dominant paradigm of the day (Kuhn, 1970), with radically new conceptualizations being rare. This, of course, contributes to relative cultural stability.

Thus, the language of a culture provides a person with a conceptual system within which to explain events or to frame perceptions. That the individual normally understands any given phenomenon in terms of the conceptual system available through the culture has become generally accepted. Bruner (1980) has, however, recently suggested that the influences of a culture may transcend its linguistic system:

> What language permits is a rapid and easy mode of access into a huge array of data, concepts, and conceptual procedures, right from the start of one's career as a member of the linguistic community. It *may* be that creatures without language could, under favorable (manmade?) circumstances, come to grasp comparably complex and powerful concepts. Their mode of access, however, would be so slow and so demanding of concentration and time that they would have to be intellectual saints to make it, renouncing most of the more primitive biological needs and satisfactions en route!
>
> It seems, however, that human cultures do more than equip their members with skills and concepts and views about the world and life. They also have an effect—a differential one—on the ways in which their members *use mind.* This is a topic that is only beginning to come under study. (p. 382–383)

It is probably the case that there is much yet to learn about cultural meaning systems. This includes the effects that existing cultures have on the manner in which the infant learns to utilize his or her mind as well as the ways in which shared meaning systems are negotiated and transmitted. Since it is through participation in the culture that human beings are able to function within social systems, this is critical knowledge for the clinical social worker.

Cultural Diversity and Identity Complexity

So far in this discussion culture has often been referred to as if it were a singular and static thing. It is not. Culture, like individual meaning systems, is a dynamic and changing thing that needs constant maintenance:

> The range of examples suggests, as I mean it to, that people create culture continuously. Since no two situations are alike, the cultural solutions available to them are only approximate. Even in the simplest societies, no two people learn quite the same cultural material; the chance encounters of daily life provide sufficient variation to ensure

that. No set of cultural understandings, then provides a perfectly applicable solution to any problem people have to solve in the course of their day, and they therefore must remake those solutions, adapt their understandings to the new situation in the light of what is different about it. Even the most conscious and determined effort to keep things as they are would necessarily involve strenuous efforts to remake and reinforce understandings so as to keep them intact in the face of what was changing. (Becker, 1986, p. 19)

Some degree of cultural stability is undoubtedly necessary in order for people to be able to share in its meaning systems. But even in simple societies changes in the physical environment alone require the creation of new knowledge.

The developed Western countries, however, are not simple societies; they are multicultural, composed of myriad diverse groups. The United States is rapidly becoming the most ethnically diverse of all of these societies (Comas-Diaz & Griffith, 1988). In the past, even theories on the acculturation of immigrant groups have tended to imply that ethnic diversity means there are isolated pockets in a society within which immigrants subscribe to a different but uniform culture, and from which their children dissociate into the general "melting pot" culture, which is presumably also uniform.

Some of the recent literature on minority groups has suggested viewing the members of these groups as individuals who must belong to and participate in two cultures (Chestang, 1979; Lukes & Land, 1990). While this is a useful perspective, pointing out that for effective social functioning members of minority groups often need a more highly developed capacity to create meaning than do members of majority groups, it may distract from the fact that members of traditionally disadvantaged minority groups are by no means the only persons in society who must participate in more than one culture. When culture is understood in Becker's terms— as a constantly changing meaning system through which people coordinate their activities—it becomes clear that even in very simple societies there is some degree of cultural diversity.

Every human group within which a person may participate develops its own shared meaning system for dealing with the coordination of its activities. The individual normally participates in many different groups—for example, nuclear family, extended family, groups organized around a variety of activities that involve both work and recreation, groups that may be organized around age or sex membership, and groups espousing formalized belief systems. In a complex society the individual normally participates in a number of somewhat different cultures or shared meaning systems in the course of an average day.

A decision about what is considered appropriate behavior in any given group depends on an understanding of the culture of that particular group, including its views on the status, role, and function of its members. Belonging to more than one group at any time increases the possibility that the cultural prescriptions of one group may be proscribed by another. Memberships in multiple groups increases the possibility of conflict for the individual, since behavioral prescriptions of different groups may be at variance with one another. It is probable that healthy individuals resolve these conflicts through the construction of a kind of hierarchical organization of varying allegiances to these prescriptions. It is not inconceivable, however, that there may be a maximum number of groups with which any individual can feel a sense of identification while retaining the ability to integrate the various aspects of these identifications into an organized identity system.

While conflicts over allegiance to differing meaning systems resulting from participation in differing cultures can play some part in problems in psychological or social functioning, the role of inner conflict in the production of such problems has been overestimated from the days of Freud's early theories. After pointing out the possibilities for conflict, Allen, Wilder, and Atkinson (1983) note the following advantages to membership in multiple groups:

> Having a large number of group memberships is not without its advantages, however. Membership in a large number of groups offers an individual the possibility of alternate sources of positive social identity when membership in one important group is lost or if it is downgraded; these alternative resources would be less likely to be utilized in a simpler group membership system. Furthermore, evidence suggests that the membership in a more differentiated social environment may be positively related to social adjustment and the ability to deal effectively with problems in everyday life. Cognitive flexibility and the ability to adapt to situational contingencies are acquired in the course of the frequent modulations of social identity that occur when multiple group membership exists. (p. 97)

The fact that multiple group membership contributes to cognitive flexibility can be understood as the result of participation in a variety of worldviews and culturally based problem-solving patterns. Thus, the person with identity complexity can be expected to have a broader array of conceptual resources available to maintain effective social functioning.

Identity complexity and an appreciation for the diversity of cultural meaning systems are highly important for any individual's ability to function effectively in society. These things are also essential for the clinical social worker. Without an awareness of the diversity of meaning systems it can be easy for the clinician to mistake a client's lack of awareness of or lack of subscription to some aspect of the dominant culture for a lack of ability to create meaning.

II THE PROCESSES OF THE SELF

5 Internalization

Internalization is the activity through which the individual builds an inner world. It is one of the two major groups of processes of the self, the other being that of regulation (which is addressed in Chapter 6). Since internalization is the process through which identity is acquired, understanding its nature is extremely important for any clinical theory. Yet there have been many problems involving concepts of internalization in traditional clinical theories.

Freud used the term *internalization* infrequently in his writings. This hardly seems surprising given the fact that one of the central tenets of his theory involved the acquisition of ultimate meaning not through interaction in the environment but through biological inheritance. Perhaps the fact that Freud still needed a concept of internalization, even with the idea of inherited meaning, is an indication of the inadequacy of seeing meaning as derived from the drives.

It is one of many complex contradictions within Freud's writing that he developed a theory of internalization, which can also be seen as a theory of cognition (Rapaport, 1951). The fundamental premise of the theory is that the infant evokes an internal hallucination of the object, initially the breast, in order to defend against the annihilation anxiety that is aroused by the loss of the breast. Thus, the basic purpose of internalization is a defense against feelings of loss, and it is the inevitability of loss that motivates the development and utilization of a conceptual world.

In "Mourning and Melancholia" Freud (1915) extended this idea of internalization as a defense against feelings of loss to an explanation of the difference between normal mourning and psychotic depression. In psychotic depression the loss is experienced as a loss of a part of the self whereas in normal mourning internalization allows the person to retain a substitute for the lost object (an idea that Lindemann, 1965, later expanded). The idea that a highly developed representational world makes the normal mourning of losses possible is a useful one. However, as Loewald (1973) suggested, positing defense as the motivation for all cognitive functioning is problematic in that it leaves little room for notions of healthy curiosity, creativity, or mastery.

Hartmann (1958; Hartmann & Loewenstein, 1962) paid considerable attention to the notion of internalization. He essentially depathologized internalization by seeing it as motivated by pleasure in functioning rather than as a defense against feelings of loss. For Hartmann, however, what was internalized was psychic structure—ego and superego structures. This implies a relationship between psychic structure and cognition, a concept probably derived from the influence of Piaget's work on Hartmann; however, Hartmann never fully addressed this relationship.

In *The Self and the Object World,* Jacobson (1964) provided a detailed description of mother–infant interactions through which the child was assumed to build a representational world involving both self and object. She made no attempt to locate the processes she described within a social or cultural context and was critical of some aspects of Erikson's concept of identity. Nevertheless, Jacobson's representational world is much more satisfying as an interactive theory of cognition than is Freud's in spite of its remaining within the language of drive theory, though departing somewhat from Freudian theory in the area of affect.

Classical drive theory uses a number of words referring to internalization processes: *incorporation, introjection,* and *identification,* as well as *internalization.* This vocabulary reflects the fact that the process of internalization was expected to vary in accordance with the characteristics of the psychosexual stage in which it occurred. Thus, for example, incorporation and introjection were normally considered to be oral processes whereas identification was the internalization process associated with the more developmentally advanced oedipal stage. Through an understanding of these associations a therapist could know the level of pathology in the adult since each level had a characteristic form of internalization.

There was considerable variation in the manner in which the classical terms for internalization processes were defined. As a result, there were a number of attempts to clarify psychoanalytic theory in this regard, the last of these probably being written by Meissner (1981). Of these psychoanalytic works on internalization the most widely read and quoted has been Schafer's (1968) *Aspects of Internalization.* Yet within a few years of the publication of this book Schafer disclaimed his ideas entirely (Schafer, 1976). Prominent among his arguments against the psychoanalytic concept of internalization was his charge that it was based on a conception of psychological processes that was both anthropomorphic and teleologic. That is, it gave the impression that there were a host of people who had been orally absorbed into the individual's inner world and who influenced actions from that vantage point.

Behind the assumption that there is a world of objects inside the individual, one finds drive theory's assumption about accurate perceptions and its failure to deal with created meaning. As Stern (1985) has pointed out, what is internalized is not the object per se but, rather, the experience with the object. It is a testament to the pervasiveness of the 19th-century scientific point of view within mainstream psychoanalytic theory that the idea of the internalization of the object should have remained influential for so long. In 1953 Sullivan wrote the following:

> The idea that one can, in some way, take in another person to become part of one's personality is one of the evils that comes from overlooking the fact that between a doubtless real "external object" and a doubtless real "my mind" there is a group of processes—the act of perceiving, understanding, and what not—which is intercalated, which is highly subject to past experience and increasingly subject to foresight of the neighboring future. Therefore, it would in fact be one of the greatest miracles of all time if our perception of another person were, in any significant number of respects, accurate or exact. (p. 167)

In a recent article on internalization that appears in the relatively conservative *Psychoanalytic Study of the Child,* Behrends and Blatt (1985) agree with Stern's position that what is internalized is the experience rather than the object. They also point out that the child is motivated by attempts to organize experience. Furthermore, they suggest that the process of internalization does not vary in accordance with the psychosexual stage of the individual.

For purposes of the theory under consideration here, the idea that what is internalized is the experience has critically important implications. First, it explains that there is a difference between interaction as the objectively viewed activity between two persons and the relationship between those two persons, which includes the shared meaning of that interaction. When applied to the clinical situation this distinction can be understood to mean that in attempting to create a relationship with a client the clinical social worker is helping the client participate in a shared meaning system. If it is also understood that the goal of treatment is to help enable the client to participate in the shared meaning system called culture, the therapeutic purpose of a clinical relationship is clarified.

Additionally, understanding what is internalized as the experience with the object provides a basis for making a distinction between the meaning involved in a relationship and the causally based effects, either healthy or pathological, of an interaction on the ability to create meaning. The mother of the client who claims to have had a good relationship with her may ultimately be considered to have had a pathological influence; conversely, the mother of the client who reports a negative relationship may have encouraged considerable health. The content of the meaning created in or about an interpersonal interaction must be considered separately from the effect of that relationship on the capacity to create meaning. As will be seen, this applies not only to interactions that occur with significant others outside of the treatment setting but inside it as well.

Furthermore, since the concept of internalization interposes meaning between the internal world of the person and interactions within the external world, it helps to explain how it is that the individual can achieve identity complexity. Not only does the individual have experiences with a variety of different significant others (Emde, 1981) but even the individual whose experience of different objects is not extensive has many different types of experience with the same person.

Finally, the idea that what is internalized is the experience with the object rather than the object itself opens the door for a theory in which the relationship between the intrapsychic world of the individual and the shared meaning system that is the culture can be explained. It becomes possible to reconcile clinical theory with the ideas of Parsons (1964), who indicated that what was internalized was the culture, and Vygotsky (1962), who believed that all that is internal was once external. This reconciliation is possible because the individual's experience is not merely with isolated human beings as objects but with a world that includes a social structure and a physical environment as well as other humans.

Memory

Ideas about the nature of memory are central to understanding the nature of internalization processes and of the content that is internalized. Without memory, human beings would have no sense of organization across time or of endurance, which, as Erikson (1980) emphasized in his concept of identity, is extremely important for psychological health. Loewald (1980b) has attributed the experience of fragmentation of the self to an inability to order a given event in a context of the present, past, and future, with the result that the moment stands alone, not embedded in a time continuum. The temporal ordering of experience is a basic and critical function for human beings.

Within clinical theory there has been considerable debate about whether therapy is or should be focused on an understanding of the past or of the "here and now." This argument, however, seems to be based on the misconception that time unfolds in a simple linear fashion (Modell, 1990). As long ago as St. Augustine (Polkington, 1988), it was recognized that the past, as well as the future, dwells in the present. There is a present about the future—expectation—and a present about the past—memory—as well as a present about the present. Memory is not just content but is also an activity (Loewald, 1976), and while the content is concerned with the past, memorial activity always occurs in the present.

Freud not only believed that perception was accurate, rather like a photograph, but he also thought that anything that had been perceived was forever recorded in memory, that the individual's ability to recall accurately what occurred at earlier times in life could be restored through psychoanalysis, and that this restoration was central to treatment efficacy. The memory might be conscious or unconscious, depending on whether or not it could be put into language (Freud, 1914). For Freud, then, memory was not an activity but more of a static recording of content from events past.

However, Piaget's (1962) assumption that the infant begins life only with patterns of action makes it possible to understand that some experiences that affect the individual may be recorded strictly in action patterns. Memory in the form of action patterns has normally been called "enactive memory" and is clinically important because it underlies repetition compulsion and transference phenomena (Saari, 1986). Enactive memory, as well as imagistic memory, can also be seen to compose meaning that has not been constructed into conscious symbolically based meaning systems.

Freud's notion of memory as an accurate recording of events is, of course, no longer tenable (Cohler, 1982). Cofer (1977), for example, has noted that a person constructs an interpretation of perceptual input on the basis of the interaction of contextual factors and existing knowledge. The individual, then, is an active participant in the memorial undertaking, from comprehension to retention, utilizing the framework provided by her or his schemata for dealing with the world in general. That is, memories are constructed just as is the rest of the individual's knowledge of the world.

The format in which memory content is recorded has been a matter of considerable psychological research. It is now generally agreed that seven, the number of digits in local telephone numbers, is about the maximum number of unrelated items that can readily be recalled by the normal human mind. Research has indicated that the number of items that can be recalled becomes significantly greater if the items can be placed within categories. For example, a person is more likely to remember the names of a number of fruits if these are first divided into categories according to the color of the fruit.

However, Mandler (1984) has recently pointed out that more can be readily recalled if they are arranged within stories than if they are in purely taxonomical categories. Furthermore, recall of simple stories by adults, from nonliterates to the college-educated, seems to vary little with education. In fact, creating a story about nonnarrative material is a common and successful method for improving the ability to recall the material.

Mandler provides a couple of explanations as to why stories should be easier to recall. She believes that stories have an underlying structure that can be grasped almost immediately whereas lists require first a recognition of the category involved. She also notes, as have a number of other authors (e.g., Polkington, 1988), that story structures seem to be the same across cultures, even though the content of the stories may vary considerably. Thorndyke (1977) found that the comprehension and recall of stories were related to the amount of inherent story structure and that this was independent of the actual content of the story passage.

In addition to her observations about story structure, Mandler notes that in taxonomical categories the relationships are vertical, in the sense that there is a hierarchical abstraction among the categories. For example, maple and pine can be classified as types of wood and wood itself might be categorized as a type of material from which furniture can be constructed. Classification systems contain vertical relationships through the matrix of categories into which the various words can be related. On the other hand, stories can reflect much more complex relationships easily, since in addition to the vertical relationships there are also horizontal ones that relate to the time line or coexistence of items. Ideas about a choice of furniture made from either maple or pine might be embedded within a story about newlyweds furnishing their first home.

Clearly, human memory is captured in some sort of organization. Increasingly, evidence is mounting in support of the thesis that narrative is a metacode within which humans universally organize and transmit information (Polkington, 1988; White, 1980). It is reasonable to think, therefore, that the basic structure of cognition and memory must be one that would underlie the organization of material in a narrative form. Identity has also been observed to occur in narrative form. It is the stories we tell to and about ourselves that makes up our sense of who we are (Mancuso & Sarbin, 1983).

Event Representation

Current psychodynamic theory assumes that the need to organize experience is fundamental for human beings. Organization must, of course, occur through or within some sort of structure. To date, the basic conceptual structure available for use in such organization has been assumed to be that of abstract taxonomic categories. Piaget's work (1962) focused on formulating an explanation of how knowledge through the use of such categories is possible. In the years since Piaget's brilliant work, however, a number of studies have shown that children have conceptual abilities that are not reflected in Piaget's experiments (see, for example, Donaldson, 1978). As a result of such findings, the past 10 to 15 years have seen work on conceptualization that is revolutionary for an understanding of the basic form of internal structures.

One of the new conceptualizations is that of amodal perception, which Stern (1985) has described in terms of infants' experiencing a world of perceptual unity by perceiving qualities in any perceptual form (sound, sight, smell, touch, etc.) and transforming them into other modalities. In the past, perception was usually studied in terms of the specific modality utilized, an approach that raised the question of how the brain related various perceptions to one another. Positing the existence of a perceptual unity from the outset has basically bypassed this problem.

Another important new idea, described by Stern (1985), is the "episode," or basic unit of memory. While there is controversy in the literature on the precise dimensions of an episode, it is defined as a small unit of experience as it has been lived. Recall is expected to be of the episode as a whole, that is, the event itself, the perceptions of the external setting, the internal emotional context, the bodily sensations and/or actions, and the cognitions involved. Taken together, amodal perception and episodic memory provide a basis for a revolutionary, holistic way of approaching human psychological functioning.

Katherine Nelson (1986) warns that this view of perception does not mean that percepts of the external world are "accurate" or "truthful":

> An important point highlighted by the consideration of immediate perception as an initial representation is that cognitive processes such as categorization, pattern analysis, inference, and so on, operate not on real world phenomena but only on the mental representation of those phenomena. . . . perception of an event is strongly determined by expectations, by prior schemas, and by other cognitive and affective states. . . . The constraint works both ways: the initial perception of an event is constrained by prior knowledge, and the acquisition of new knowledge is constrained by initial perceptual representation. The constraints are not complete, of course, or no change of any kind in the system could take place. (p. 7)

Nelson points out that cognitive processes cannot operate on what has not initially been represented through perception.

Initial perceptions, then, are contextually constrained and individually constructed. What cognitive operations are then carried out on these perceptions? According to Stern (1989a), the infant puts together a series of episodes to form a working model or script. The idea of scripts was apparently originated by Shank and Abelson (1977), who thought of a script as an ordered sequence of actions organized around a goal and appropriate to a particular spatiotemporal context. A script specifies the actors, actions, and props that are necessary to carry out the goals involved.

A script about eating in a restaurant would involve waitpersons, ordering food, tables, menus, and bills. These items are assumed to exist in any restaurant script, so that even if they are not specifically mentioned in a story involving a restaurant, the individual with knowledge of that script will assume them. Some items in a script are presumed to be optional whereas others are obligatory.

For example, ordering dessert in a restaurant is optional, paying the bill is not. A script is temporally ordered. In some scripts, for example, a restaurant script, there is a necessary arrangement to this order; one must order the food before one can eat it.

Scripts, it should be noted, provide culturally specific knowledge. Anyone familiar with current American culture would immediately know that some restaurants, especially fast-food ones, in fact do not involve waiters or waitresses but, rather, counters at which to order and obtain the food. In clinical work it is not uncommon when a client describes a troublesome social encounter for the clinician to ask a question that calls attention to some important aspect of the situation that the client failed either to perceive or to attribute appropriate significance to. It is the knowledge that comes not from an accurate perception of reality but from culturally shared scripts that enables the clinician to do this. What has been called intuition in clinical work is probably often based on the use of inferential processes within script knowledge. Such intuition, then, will not work nearly as well if client and clinician participate in different cultures and the script knowledge is not socially shared. This may not prevent effective therapy, but it will mean that both parties will have to work harder in their communication.

Scripts integrate into one structure knowledge about objects and their relations and knowledge about the world of people and their interactions. A recognition of scripts is a new conceptual achievement, since previous theories of cognition, with the notable exception of Vygotsky (1962), have focused on internal individual processes in a vacuum. According to Nelson (1986):

> A model of cognitive development that fails to consider the mechanisms by which the child incorporates knowledge gained from and within social interactive situations is inadequate to most of the problems that such a model needs to address. . . . Social interactions are as much a part of such events as the physical objects that are embedded within them. In fact, objects take on meaning only within events. (p. 240)

At the same time, the fact that the script is based on cultural knowledge does not wholly determine individual experiences, which vary considerably.

Nelson (1886) and her colleagues have utilized the idea of scripts in their formulation of event representations, which they believe to be basic to the manner in which children build a representational world. Their research has indicated that children as young as 3 years can provide a generalized report of the sequence of events at an occasion such as a birthday party even if they have only experienced one such occasion. The children may neglect to mention all the possible occurrences but will invariably report correctly the sequence of the ones they do recall.

An event representation is an abstraction from the experience of events and not a simple reflection of these events. Children are able to achieve the construction of an event representation even if they have not directly experienced the event. This is possible because of exposure to the event in the cultural media, such as television. When asked to tell a story, very young children will frequently recount a temporally ordered script, for example, about what happens when eating in a restaurant rather than an acount of why this particular meal was noteworthy. That is, children use event representations to construct their stories. As they grow older, the event representations become increasingly decontextualized, permitting more flexibility, and their stories acquire an evaluative dimension.

Both Mandler (1984) and Nelson (1986) and her colleagues assume that event representations, rather than object representations, are the fundamental building blocks of thinking. Mandler notes that in stories, scripts, and scenes (spatially based organizations of objects) the relationship to abstraction is that of part to whole. For example, in a kitchen scene a dishwasher would be one part of the whole. This part/whole relationship is easier to grasp and utilize than is the abstraction of an aspect or quality upon which categorical conceptualization is based. According to Nelson, preschool children make extensive use of event representations, but symbolic ability based on taxonomic categories does not begin before 6 or 7 years of age. The assumption here is that event representations form the basis from which higher level cognitive operations such as taxonomic categories and notions of causality are derived.

A script contains a number of slots into which different items or "slot fillers" can be placed. For example, in a restaurant script the waitperson can be either a waiter or a waitress and the menu might list hamburgers or steaks. Early knowledge of conceptual categories can then be seen to derive from the child's grasp of the various items that can be placed within a particular slot without violating the integrity of the script's meaning. Later the child may learn to identify the particular aspect that, when abstracted, fulfills the requirements of the particular slot in question, for example, food that may be ordered in a restaurant. Complex relational language eventually becomes mapped onto the knowledge that the child already has from event representations.

The earliest form of humor observed in young children involves practicing with the relative appropriateness or inappropriateness of particular items as slot fillers. For example, a young child might declare that there was an elephant eating dinner at Johnny's house and find the ridiculousness of such an idea tremendously amusing. In this and similar examples, however, what the child is actually doing is mastering notions of both categories and social situations by determining which items are acceptable slot fillers.

Nelson (1985) explains how event representations explain some of the findings contradicting Piaget's work:

> With the assumption that the event structure, not the object structure, is primary, it becomes clear why function or action should be important to the child's formation of concepts and thus to early word meanings. It is not simply because the child's own actions are fundamentally defining (as one reading of Piaget would suggest), but because conceptual representation is in the first instance the representation of event structures and objects are known in their relation to the events of which they are a part. That is, the actions of others or the event the object enters into are as important to the establishment of the object concept as are the child's own actions, so long as they are viewed as essential to the ER [event representation]. (p. 189)

From one perspective, Piaget, who introduced to psychology the idea of the importance of action, can be seen not to have taken this idea far enough in regard to its presence in the child and in the social context as well.

Event representations are social in two senses. They are acquired through interactive experiences, and they provide shared meaning that can serve as a guide for behavior in similar situations:

> Finally, it should be stressed also that because ERs (event representations) serve as the basis for action and participation, they guarantee at least a minimum of *shared* interpretation with other people. Although the child's representation of the activity may differ in ways from the parent's, their expectations for each other in well-practiced routines constitute *shared knowledge* and thus form the basis for the establishment of *shared meaning.* (Nelson, 1985, p. 188)

There may, however, be considerable variation in the degree of generalizability of the shared meaning of an event representation.

Normally, families are expected to serve a socializing role in preparing the child to function within the surrounding culture. However, studies of severely disturbed families (Lidz, Fleck & Cornelison, 1965) long ago pointed out that some children acquire expectations about the world that are adaptive within the limited sphere of their nuclear family but maladaptive in the rest of the world.

For clinical social workers, understanding that internalization occurs through event representation is extremely important and confirming of the profession's traditional stance regarding the person/situation configuration. Not only is the internalized content of the event representation based on the social context but the conditions of the social context make internalization possible as well. Nelson (1986) made the following observations:

> A child who faces a world that is constantly changing, that does not provide the kind of repeatable event structure that makes a stable event representation possible, cannot achieve this kind of stability. We call this the *chaos factor* and speculate that it may have broad repercussions for the impairment of cognitive functioning when stable representations are not established and thus do not become available for cognitive processing. (pp. 246–247)

Thus, the conditions, both social and physical, existing in the environment can have an influence on the development of the individual's capacity to create meaning, that is, on the development of the processes of the self.

The content of event representations which is based on experiences with the child's environment, can be seen to provide the initial foundation for identity. There is unquestionably much more to be learned about the construction of identity from this perspective. However, one early study has yielded some interesting results. Nelson (1989c) and associates placed, with the knowledge and cooperation of the parents, a tape recorder underneath the crib of a somewhat precocious young girl, Emily, from the ages of 21 to 36 months, and tape-recorded both her bedtime dialogues with her parents and her monologues to herself before falling asleep. The authors interpret their findings to indicate that the primary use this child made of her monologue was to create representations of her everyday experiences and the world around her.

Interestingly, Emily used more highly developed speech patterns in her monologues to herself than she did in the dialogues with her parents. The parents tended to focus frequently on events that were expected to occur after Emily woke up. Although at times, Emily referred in her monologues to the content of the dialogues with her parents, for the most part she talked not about the future but, rather, about what had already occurred. In her monologues she appears to be trying to master her understanding of how the world around her works. In other words, Emily seemed to be constructing event representations.

During the time period of the tape-recording Emily experienced the birth of a younger brother. This event certainly had a major effect on her life, especially since she was moved to another bedroom further away from her parents' in anticipation of her sibling's arrival. Classical psychoanalytic theory suggests that this experience ought to have a major impact on a child. Yet it is hardly mentioned in Emily's monologues. The monologues focus on everyday routines rather than on major life changes such as a sibling's birth. From a perspective of traditional psychodynamic theory this is somewhat surprising.

The fact that Emily did not talk about her brother very much does not, of course, mean that her brother's birth did not have a significant impact on her, but it does signal the wisdom of caution in making assumptions about what historical life events may mean to a client in the absence of evidence from that client. Further, it suggests that perhaps the very young child needs to be able to construct an understanding of the expectable in the world in order to have a cognitive context within which to understand the meaning of particularly significant events. If the child has been unable to construct reliable event representations, it may be difficult or impossible for the child to comprehend the meaning of more major and significant single occurrences.

The studies on event representations indicate that they both contribute to autobiographical memory and tend to distort it in ways that are important for the clinical social worker to know. Many clinicians are alerted to the idea that clients may not think to report unusual aspects of their family life because abstractions from their own experience led to the unexamined assumption that this aspect was the same in all families. An understanding of event representations, of course, explains this. What may be more surprising, however, is that since common occurrences tend to become generalized into a script, the memories for specific episodes tend to be of the ones that are atypical. Thus, while the client who was frequently beaten by her father may neglect to mention this, the client who has a distinct and affectively invested memory of having been hit may well have experienced this only once.

Autobiographical memory is a combination of generalized-event knowledge and specific episodes, but these may become fused with each other in the construction of the representation. If not all aspects of the specific episode have been perceived, a common element from event knowledge may be inaccurately used to fill in the gap. Conversely, memory of a specific episode can become confused with similar experiences and the generalizations that may be based on them. An understanding of the functioning of event knowledge therefore calls into serious question the accuracy of autobiographical memory; clinical theories of etiology based on client memory are highly questionable.

Conditions within the social and physical environment of the individual can stimulate a high level of development of the processes of the self or result in a relative lack of development. However, the specific content of any individual's memory or identity system is not a reliable indicator of the causal factors involved in the relative development of the capacity to create meaning.

6 Regulation

Regulation is the second of the two major groups of processes of the self. The self is conceived of as an activity, not a state or a developmental level that, once achieved, remains basically functional for the remainder of the individual's life. The self is constantly in operation, selecting and processing input and integrating this new information into the content of older meaning systems. Regulation consists of the activity directed toward the retention of sufficient organization so that the internalizing activity upon which purposeful behavior depends can continue.

Although Freud's (1920) definition of pleasure as a lack of tension and his proposal that a stimulus barrier exists at birth to protect the child from the anxiety of excessive stimulation have now been discredited, it is clear that the human organism has neither limitless energy nor the ability to deal endlessly with stimulation without the experience of disorganization. Hebb (1949) found that what would be experienced as pleasurable varies with the energic level of the organism; that is, in some states a lack of tension is experienced as pleasure, but at other times stimulation is pleasurable. At the extremes of either too much stimulation or of a lack of stimulation, there is a strain on the functioning of the self and a state of fragmentation or disorganization may threaten functional capability.

In the past the idea of regulative activity has been commonly used in understanding both human physiology and psychology. However, because of the dominance of a drive psychology paradigm this regulation has been primarily seen in terms of levels of physiologic activity related to states of sexual excitation or affect discharge. When one accepts a theory in which meaning as an intervening variable between physiology and behavior is considered essential, it becomes clear that regulation preserves the capacity to create meaning through the activity of internalization.

When conditions conducive to maximal functioning exist, the regulatory activities of the self serve to protect and maintain the ability to process perceptual information. When such conditions prevail in childhood, the capacity to process information through internalizing activity follows a developmental course, with the individual becoming able to handle more input and gradually to arriving at a differentiated and integrated organization in the content of the processed meaning. Under adverse conditions, however, the development of internalizing skill can be stunted, leaving the individual with a deficit in the capacity to create meaning. While deficiencies in the capacity to create meaning can occur at any time in life, the individual is most vulnerable during the early developmental years. In a similar sense, it is possible that growth in the capacity to create meaning can occur at any time in life, but its likelihood is undoubtedly greater during the first half of a normal life expectancy.

The neurologically normal infant responds differentially to stimuli that are experienced as pleasurable and those that are experienced as painful, including those stimuli that originate in contacts with others. For example, the young infant can signal through body movements or facial expressions a wish to engage in interaction with another human being or it can disengage by pulling away or averting its face. In spite of some initial ability to regulate perceptions, however, the infant needs considerable assistance in order to maintain a level of stimulation that is in concert with the internal energic state; it is the caretaking other, the selfobject (Kohut, 1984) or the self regulating other (Stern, 1985), who performs this function.

The use of self-regulating others continues throughout life, but the need for reliance on them is significantly reduced by the development of a representational world. For example, Emily, the young girl whose bedtime verbalizations were tape-recorded, seemed to enjoy being alone and using her monologues to create and master her own sense of the world around her. In the absence of perceptual stimulation from interaction with the environment, she could devote her attention to processing the perceptions that had already been registered. Through such practicing of the activities of the self not only do the internalizing processes develop the ability to handle more input but, in a coordinated fashion, the processes of the regulation of the self become able to allow for more input that is then available for processing.

The fact that the individual at times needs to be alone—or alone in the presence of others (Winnicott, 1958a)—in order to exercise meaning-making skills should not be taken to indicate that meaning making is not a social activity. As both Watson (1989) and Stern (1989) indicate, the very perceptions that Emily called up in her monologues to herself contained representations of being with others and thus mitigated her sense of being separate even though she was alone. In the absence of previous contacts with others and without an awareness of their continuing existence, Emily would be unable to create meaning when alone.

Although the development of an internalized representational world allows for lesser reliance on external conditions for self-regulation, a complete autonomy never develops. What actually occurs throughout life is an extremely complex interrelationship among the conditions of the external environment, the regulatory activity of the self, the internalization of perceptual input into the content of the representational world, and the nature of the content of that representational world.

The Transitional Self

The regulatory activities of the self occur in two different spheres. In an earlier attempt at capturing the complexities of the human meaning system, I suggested that the self was divided into the transitional and operational selves (Saari, 1986). In the present work these terms are being retained, though with a somewhat refined conceptualization. As used here, the transitional self involves the regulatory activities that control the level of perceptual input that is allowed to be registered through internalization. An open or closed boundary of the transitional self, then, refers to the relative level of regulation of perceptual input. The basis of the transitional self is present at birth in the infant's ability to engage or disengage with the self-regulating other.

The concept of boundaries of the self essentially utilizes a spatial metaphor. There are dangers involved in a too literal use of such a metaphor. Indeed, in different ways Schafer (1976), Loewald (1962), and Palombo (1987) have all commented on difficulties involved in conceiving of the self within a spatial metaphor. The origin of such a metaphor is Winnicott's (1965) assertion that the self cannot function either when fused with or in isolation from others, an understanding that has increasingly been seen as useful within theories of psychotherapy (Modell, 1990). The idea that the individual must modulate "interpsychic space" in order to avoid either merger or isolation has also been proposed (Saari, 1986).

The idea of interpsychic space relates to the need to regulate the periods of interactive contact with others and is compatible with Winnicott's use of a spatial metaphor to describe the modulation of psychological closeness/distance between the self and others. However, from a theoretical perspective it is important to keep in mind that although the regulatory activities carried out through the boundaries of the transitional self are experienced as determining the degree of social connectedness of the individual, both that which is regulated and that which does the regulating are activities rather than spaces.

The functioning of the boundaries of the transitional self is intimately connected with the communicative function of meaning, which at the beginning of life is manifested by facial expressions and develops into experientially differentiated categorical emotions such as mad, sad, glad, and scared. The individual, of course, is ordinarily aware only of the affective state, not its regulative function. The man who becomes angry with his "nagging" wife may not be aware either of his anger as an attempt to get psychological distance or of the function of this distance in preserving his capacity to create his own meaning. As Seton (1981) has noted,

> It has not been possible to speak entirely separately of the parts played by affect in influencing the spatial dimension of object relations, its part in affirming or denying one's social connectedness and its part in the individual's experience of self, because affects are not experienced that way. Instead, individual and social aspects of affect experience are interdependent, though their mix varies greatly. (p. 10)

In the initial days of life the regulation carried out by the transitional self is an instinctive and biologically based response. While this response is a reaction to the meaning of an interaction with the environment, it is not processed through a meaning system. Throughout life this type of reflex-like reaction continues to operate, for example, in the almost automatic response to a loud noise. In other words, the reactions of the boundaries of the transitional self are often, but not always, based on evaluations of meaning of which the individual is unconscious.

Although the reactions of the boundaries of the transitional self are initially physiologically based and nonconscious, such reactions do become conditioned or habituated through repeated experience. For example, an adult woman whose sexually abusive father always wore red pajamas when he came to her childhood room at night may become psychologically frozen in the presence of a man wearing red without having any conscious knowledge of why this occurs. In this case the concept of the color red has not become fully differentiated from the event representation of father coming to the bedroom and therefore signals that event. While such unconscious regulations may sometimes be a part of a pathological pattern, they frequently contribute greatly to the preservation of adequate functioning through the anticipation of commonly occurring events.

In the aforementioned example, the boundaries of the transitional self close on the basis of an evaluative judgment about the meaning of the perceptions for the safety of the self. The safety of the self may be experienced as threatened, however, not only by judgments about the qualitative meaning of perceptions but also by a quantitive excess of stimulation. The capacity to create meaning is one of the many biologically based functions that require contact with other human beings in order to develop properly (Ainsworth, Blehar, Waters, & Wall, 1978; Bowlby, 1969). Contact with another human being provides a powerful stimulus to this function, a stimulus that is necessary and yet that at times can also be so strongly experienced that it can threaten to overload the capacity. Stimulus overload can, of course, lead to a state of experienced disorganization and fragmentation.

For the sexually abused woman mentioned earlier, a man wearing red may signal such excessive danger that it is not possible for her to relate to him, even though he may be entirely unlike her father. The boundaries of the transitional self simply shut down the registering of perceptions. Although this perceptual blocking is clearly not what Freud meant by the term *denial*, Basch (1988) has defined denial in this way. (See also Blatt and Wild, 1976, for additional discussion of perceptual boundaries.) When denial occurs and perceptions are not registered, the information contained in these perceptions is not available for any further processing within the meaning system; it is information that is unconscious in the sense that it is simply not available to the individual.

Under conditions that are optimal for functioning, the boundaries of the self remain flexibly responsive to the nature of the surrounding environment. Thus, they will be relatively open to input from others experienced as friendly, and relatively closed to input from those who are experienced as hostile or dangerous. The development of such flexibility, however, would appear to depend on a life experience that includes a mix of both the friendly and the hostile, but with a predominance of the friendly. An environment in which negative experiences predominate can lead to boundaries that are rigidly closed to input or to a state of hyperalertness for certain stimuli that signal danger and a tendency to disregard other types of information. In a similar sense, an environment that provides little stimulation may lead to boundaries that are perpetually too open.

The transitional self, then, can be seen to regulate both the relative level of perceptual input that is registered for further processing by the internalizing activities and the degree of psychological closeness or distance between the individual and others.

The Operational Self

The sphere of regulation of the processing of already registered perceptions is called the *operational self.* The operational self protects the internalizing activities from disorganization through overload or understimulation. The relationship between the transitional and the operational selves is reciprocal. When the boundaries of the transitional self are permitting perceptions, the internalizing function of the self is also activated. The operational self must then monitor the level of internalizing activity so that its organizational capability does not become overstressed. If a level of disorganization unacceptable to the operational self occurs, the boundaries of the transitional self will close. If the internalizing activity has insufficient input, the boundaries of the transitional self will open.

What the "self-regulating other" actually regulates in the meaning system is the level of internalizing activity of the self. For example, a soothing self-regulating other will cause the activity level to slow down while an other who is being exciting will increase that level. Both soothing and exciting can be experienced as pleasurable, but both can also be experienced as painful. The manner in which the other will be experienced is dependent upon the energy level of the organism as a biological unit. For example, another person's attempts to soothe may be experienced as painfully intrusive if the individual is needing to sleep or may be experienced as painfully unempathic if the individual is in need of increased stimulation and activity.

The fact that the affective state of the individual is affected by the relationship of the level of stimulation to the level of available energy makes it clear that the experiences to which the concept of affect has traditionally referred are not as simple or as singular as has been assumed. The affective state is essentially a reflection of an evaluation, either conscious or unconscious, of the well-being of the organism. However, there is a basic difference as to whether this evaluation is in regard to the regulation of energic levels available for the continuation of meaning making or to the implications of the content of created meaning for the relative safety of the self.

If optimum conditions for functioning and development obtain, the operational self becomes increasingly able both to allow the expenditure of more energy in the internalizing activities and to tolerate more potential disorganization before needing a reduction of the perceptual input for processing. Thus, there is the development of the phenomenon that Krystal (1988) has referred to as "affect tolerance." The individual with increased affect tolerance can handle more demand for the creation of meaning from the environment and can handle more ambiguity or conflict in the content of the meaning that has been created.

The individual with affect tolerance, who can process input at a higher activity level, also has a qualitatively different affective experience in the self. This involves a more acute sensation of the functioning of the self. Therefore, the person with more affect tolerance is likely to have what Kohut (1984) referred to as an "invigorated," as opposed to a depleted, sense of self.

The fact that a more acute sensation in the self is created by a higher level of internalizing activity also explains Winnicott's (1947) observation that hate centers the person. Actually, anger tends to cause the boundaries of the transitional self to close, but it causes the operational self to increase the expenditure of energy in the internalizing activities. Thus, the person may feel both invigorated and more organized on a short-term basis. However, if the anger becomes chronic or constantly used as a way of retaining a threatened sense of organizing ability, the individual's ability to create meaning will eventually be eroded because the boundaries of the transitional self will remain closed.

Affect, however, has been seen to be related to an evaluation not only of the quantitative level of stimulation but also to the implications of the content of created meaning for the safety of the self. In early childhood there is considerable reliance on the caretaker not just as a self-regulating other but also as one who provides cues as to the significance of environmental conditions. Noting that under circumstances of uncertainty regarding safety, infants will look to their mothers for cues as to how to behave, Emde (1989) has referred to the infants' activity as the use of social referencing.

The representational world developed through the internalizing activity of the self means that the child is less dependent upon others not just for self-regulation but for social referencing as well. As in the case of the use of self-regulating others, the human being never totally outgrows the need for social referencing. In fact, social referencing in Emde's terms is probably an early form of the kind of shared contemplation that Werner and Kaplan (1963) believed was essential to symbolizing and that, as such, was expected to be an essential activity throughout the life span. An ability to rely on the representational world to perform the evaluative function, however, does provide the individual with three distinct functional advantages.

The first of the advantages of internalized evaluation is the more efficient utilization of energy in the internalizing process. If Emily already knows that birthday parties are pleasant events at which one eats cake and ice cream, she can utilize selective attention and concentrate on clues as to when the food she enjoys is about to appear. She need not expend energy being alert to the fear of the painful needle that appears not as birthday parties, but at the doctor's office. Since there are many perceptual clues that she can now ignore as being irrelevant to the expected event of eating, the chances of her becoming overwhelmed are less.

The second of the advantages provided by an internalized representational world is regulative control over both behavior and the obtaining of need satisfaction. The growing child can, for example, increase the functioning of the transitional self through the use of the symbols available through a representational world in the regulation of communicative contact with caretakers (Watson pointed out that Emily sometimes prolonged the dialogues with her parents in order to delay separation from them).

Adults similarly utilize symbols for pragmatic communication in signaling both social and physical needs. However, the use of the representational world for evaluative purposes means that the individual can use internal decision-making processes regarding behavior rather than cues from external factors in the environment. The individual who does not have a well-developed representational world and who remains dependent on external cues will not be able to plan ahead, nor will that person be able to take advantage of past experiences. The development of a representational world allows for freedom from impulsive action. It allows the operational self to have regulative control over behavior as well as over the level of activity devoted to internalizing.

The third advantage provided by the representational world is in the experiencing of the evaluative function of affect relative to the content of the created meaning system. In other words, the individual becomes conscious of the meaning that perceptual information has for the safety of the self. While this means that the experience of conflict (or "affect intensity," as Krystal, 1988, would put it) may produce a strain on the internalizing activities, a representational world makes possible an increase in affect tolerance. It also means a considerable increase in the experience of the self as invigorated. The internalized representational world makes it possible for the operational self to permit the experiencing of a differentiated and highly articulated inner life.

Within the context of separation–individuation theory (Mahler, et al., 1975), psychological mergers, at least those beyond early childhood, have been considered to be evidence of pathology. In recent years, however, there has been much controversy over this issue, with Stern (1985) claiming that the child is born with boundaries and that a sense of merger is a developmental achievement. From the perspective presented in this book, it becomes clear that there are actually two very different types of mergers that may be experienced in adulthood.

Consider the situation in which the operational self of the individual involved is functioning well, and the evaluation of the current environment is that it is very pleasant or favorable. Under such conditions the boundaries of the transitional self become open to maximum input from the environment and the interpsychic space between the individual and the interacting other, who is experienced as a positive self-regulating other and as confirmation of a participation in the human community, becomes minimal. The pleasure from this experience is acutely felt because of the developed ability for an inner life. This type of merger is probably characteristic of moments during healthy sexual intimacy, for one example. The merger is experienced as a pleasant, global fusion and, assuming that there is no attempt to force it to last for extensive periods of time, is undoubtedly both healthy and growth producing for the individual.

Now consider the situation in which the internalizing capacity is seriously overloaded; the operational self has not functioned well enough to prevent this. The boundaries of the transitional self have not closed enough to prevent the overload. The experience of the individual is that of panic, loss of organization, and fragmentation. Instead of dealing with the excess of stimulation through a more gradually experienced closing of the interpsychic space, the operational self simply shuts off internalizing activity and the individual cannot, at least for a time, create meaning. Such an experience is assuredly not healthy or growth producing. Thus, there are two different types of merger experiences that have been described in the literature. What makes one merger healthy and the other pathologic is not necessarily the intensity of interpersonal interaction involved but, rather, is how well the operational self is functioning.

It should be apparent from the descriptions of the functioning of the operational and transitional selves that a balance between these two permits the content of the meaning systems to become increasingly differentiated and integrated. This is because there is also a relationship involving the transitional self, the operational self, and the development of the activity of internalization. In order for the development of skill in internalization, content must be available for processing at a rate that is consonant with the available energy. Internalization will proceed at an optimal rate when the transitional self is permitting sufficient input for processing and the operational self is not allowing overstimulation.

It should be noted here, however, that the homeostatic balance maintained in optimal functioning by the processes of the two selves can be envisioned as the apportionment of the level of energy available from the organism as a whole. Human physiology requires energy for operations unrelated to the creation of meaning, such as the maintenance of physical functioning, and there is a relationship between physical and mental functioning. A tired or ill person will not be able to devote his or her usual energy to the activities of the self.

In regulating the level of internalizing activity in the self and monitoring the safety of the self, then, the operational self also maintains a regulative control over impulsive behavior and establishes both the level of affect tolerance and the degree to which there will be an experienced inner life.

The Effects of Environmental Conditions

As has been seen, a balance between the transitional and operational selves is necessary for the development and facilitation of the capacity to create meaning through internalizing activity. Such a balance cannot occur unless there are human caretakers who can actively serve as self-regulating others and sources of social referencing early in the child's life and as sharers of perceptions in later stages of development. Ordinarily, clinical theory places considerable emphasis on the responsibility of caretakers for the development of the self in the child. Certainly this is a legitimate focus. On the other hand, clinical theory has frequently failed to make sufficiently clear the precise links between societal conditions beyond the family and limitations in the capacity to create meaning on the part of individuals. There are also, of course, limitations in the capacity to create meaning that have been caused by congenital deficits in the individual or by the interaction of such deficits and external conditions.

Caretakers are themselves human beings with a capacity to create meaning, the development of which has been influenced by the environmental conditions of their own lives. Caretakers who do not themselves have a highly developed meaning system will be less likely to be successful in fostering such development in others, largely because their own ability to achieve intimacy and empathic relating is limited. At the same time, the exercise of the capacity to create meaning, and ultimately the capacity itself, can be influenced either positively or negatively at any time in life. Individuals who happen to be parents or in other caretaking roles are not exempt from such influences.

The existence of a relationship between the functioning of the meaning system of the interacting caretaker and the developmental course of the child's capacity to create meaning has long been implied in psychodynamic theory. There is a current theoretical trend toward focusing more specifically on this relationship, as is apparent in such concepts as intersubjectivity (Stolorow, Brandshaft, & Atwood, 1987) and the creation of shared meaning (Schafer, 1983). In a very real sense only interaction with the mind of another human being can foster the development of a mind. From this perspective it ought to be obvious that blaming a caretaker for a failure to develop in others a capacity that they are not themselves able to exercise is truly a frustrating waste of time and effort. Conversely, helping to develop the caretaker's capacity to create meaning is very likely to help that of the child as well.

The current environment always exercises an influence on the functioning of an adult meaning system, and there is such an enormous variety of specific environmental conditions that affect this functioning that it is impossible to classify them all here. It is more important to understand that through impacting on the caretaker these conditions also influence the child. This is most obvious in the case of caretakers who have little energy to devote to the functioning of their own meaning systems. A parent who is ill or exhausted from tasks necessary for sheer physical survival will need to erect boundaries of the transitional self in order to protect whatever internalizing activity remains.

In a similar way, caretakers who evaluate the general environment as either hostile or unsafe will also normally limit boundaries. Such boundaries will, of course, mean that considerable interpsychic distance will be placed between the caretaker and the child. Insufficient stimulation of the child is likely. Often parents who normally have relatively closed boundaries genuinely want the very best for their children. Thus, they may devote considerable effort to moments of intense interaction with their children. Since it is the child's experience of the caretaker, rather than the caretaker's intentions, that influences the child's development, the result is likely to be the fostering of boundaries of the transitional self that have difficulty in maintaining a steady flow of input.

In a different type of situation, a caretaker who exists in an environment that is perhaps not evaluated as hostile but that is also not providing sufficient stimulation to maintain maximum functioning of the processes of the self is likely to utilize a relationship with a child as a source of stimulation. In such a relationship the interpsychic distance between the caretaker and the child will be determined not by the child's needs but by those of the caretaker. Excessive intrusion on the part of the caretaker, not allowing the child sufficient interpsychic distance for adequate independent processing of perceptual input, means that the child will need to erect more rigidly held boundaries as a protective maneuver. Such boundaries will then not provide the internalizing activity with enough stimulation, and a failure to develop sufficiently is likely.

While parents or immediate caretakers do have significant influence on the development of their charges, this influence is by no means solely determinative. Children, even those raised primarily within a nuclear family, interact with a variety of adults and with environmental conditions that are far beyond the control of their caretakers. Even the physical environment can have an effect on the child. Surroundings that are not attractive do not invite contemplation, and those that are barren do not invite physical activity. Under these conditions the amount of stimulation the child receives is greatly diminished.

As Nelson (1986) pointed out, young children seem to require some minimum of regular routine in daily living in order to be able to construct a representation of the world. If the environment is experienced as chaotic, the construction of an internal model on which to base expectations and behavior is much more difficult. It is likely that chronic chaos in the life of a child puts so much strain on the development of the operational self that it may be permanently impaired. Certainly, clinical evidence suggests that adults who were raised in chaotic environments are more susceptible to disorganization from current disruptions in the environment than are adults who were more fortunate as children.

As has been noted, there are many functional advantages in having a preconstructed representational world. At any time in life a significantly new environmental or cultural context, about which meaning in the form of expectations has not been preconstructed, means that the individual must attend to and process much more perceptual input and must find or invent new event representations and/or categorical systems in order to integrate this input. This situation commonly occurs, for example, when the individual moves to an unfamiliar culture (Jalali, 1988). Similarly, as Meyer (1957) pointed out, a too rapid change in any environment can result in problems in maintaining the ability to process the stimulation adequately. If the new environment is evaluated as being in some way hostile to the safety of the self, the transitional self may react with boundaries. Persistent denial can result. However, this failure to register perceptions provides no new input on which to base adjustments in the content of the meaning system. Thus, the individual may continue to be in a state of internal crisis, with no increase in the ability to function within the new environment or culture. Immigrant populations are, of course, particularly vulnerable to difficulties of this kind.

Interestingly, apparently at least some severely disturbed adolescents suffer from a similar phenomenon (Blatt & Wild, 1976; Lidz, et. al., 1965). One of the functions of the family in society is to socialize the child, that is, to teach the child about the content of the shared meaning systems in the culture. There are some families in which the parents, usually ones who are themselves suffering from impaired mental health, permit their children relatively little direct interaction with the surrounding society because they believe it to be an unsafe world. Such children may be taught a meaning system very different from the surrounding shared culture, in which they are then ill equipped to function. If, as is not uncommon, the children also come to believe that accepting a meaning system disparate from that of their parents is an act of disloyalty, the children can become both socially unskilled and severely conflicted internally.

Human beings need to be able to participate in the human community beyond their nuclear or immediate family. Erikson (1963) related this participation to late adulthood and referred to it as the achievement of generativity. It can, however, also be seen as an outgrowth of the phenomena that White (1963) termed "efficacy"—the pleasure in having an effect on the world. Normally, such pleasure can only occur if the effect on the world has some culturally determined meaning. Unfortunately, societal organization frequently makes it difficult or impossible for some individuals to participate fully.

When access to participation in the community is denied to an individual, because of ethnic, religious, or sexual differences, optimal conditions for the development and maintenance of a well-functioning meaning system simply do not exist because of a limited opportunity to utilize the activities of the self. Frequently, the denial to members of a particular group of access to participation in the community is coupled with a cultural judgment that is stereotypical and demeaning. That is, the individual is not only denied access to participation in the human community but is also provided with a negative identity. Lichtenstein (1977) has referred to this type of situation as the provision of a "malignant no."

Emily, the tape-recorded youngster, could substitute her inner world for the self-regulating functions of her parents, at least some of the time. Evidence from both the monologues and the dialogues, however, indicates that Emily experienced her parents primarily as soothing and supportive. Thus, her inner representations of her parents provided her with the soothing she needed to continue the major activity of her monologues, namely, the processing of her perceptions of the world in order to achieve an understanding of it. It is undoubtedly true that some positive experiences with the environment are essential for the development, and even the survival, of the young child.

Unfortunately, many children experience caretakers and the world around them as frightening or hostile rather than soothing a major part of the time. Clearly, in such situations energy must be invested in maintaining boundaries in the transitional self and/ or in counteracting the negative self-image in the identity content created. Little energy for the creation of meaning about other aspects of the world is left, and the self is apt to become under-developed or deficient.

Although a personal identity system can contain a wide range of content and remain perfectly functional, an identity that is consistently experienced as negative has highly debilitating effects. Since the others in the environment are expected to react with negativity to interactions, interpsychic space is apt to be consistently maintained at a distant level with considerable screening of input. At the same time, little energy is apt to be invested in internalizing activity, since there is little confidence in the ability to create a meaning system adequate for mastery of the external world. An erosion of the capacity to create meaning is the likely result.

Since the "malignant no" can be particularly devastating to the functioning of the capacity for the creation of meaning, it is not surprising that members of societal groups that experience discrimination or oppression need to form subgroups for support. The function of such groups is to provide an environment with reinforcements for a positive sense of identity, an environment within which the transitional self can allow input from the world without risking the damage of negative evaluation. Indeed, such subgroups not uncommonly even develop their own system of symbols through which to communicate (Draper, 1979), thereby de-emphasizing the meaning of the symbols from the broader culture.

The ameliorative or reparative function of support groups, either those that are naturally formed in the society or those that might be specifically formed for therapeutic purposes, can be seen to be of considerable importance in assisting the individual to develop or maintain interpsychic contact with the environment as well as to develop or maintain the ability to process input into a functional identity system. The similarity of the atmosphere in such groups to that normally encouraged in psychotherapy should be apparent.

Krystal (1988) has indicated that in states of psychic trauma the cognitive–affective meaning system of the individual simply shuts down. The person becomes numb, has essentially given up, and is vulnerable to physical as well as psychic death. He indicates that this state results from an evaluation that the threat of annihilation of the self is inescapable. What is important here is that such states in human beings occur not only when physical death appears imminent; in fact, the approach of physical death can be experienced as a psychologically meaningful event. Psychic death requires the extreme of the "malignant no" situation, that is, the unavailability of others with whom to process meaning, the influence of an environmentally imposed negative self-evaluation, and the sense of inescapability and possible physical danger.

Within any given adult population there will be considerable variation in the degree to which the capacity to create meaning exists. This capacity is influenced by a host of factors: genetically inherited potentials; physical health, including nutrition; the extent to which the interacting environment was favorable during the course of childhood development; and the current environmental conditions. While it is apparent that the capacity to create meaning can resume growth at any time in the life cycle, clinical experience indicates that some severe deficits acquired early in life are not totally reversible. As understanding of the development and functioning of the capacity to create meaning increases, so should the ability to treat such deficits. The outer limits of therapeutic effectiveness have undoubtedly not yet been established, but such may well exist.

It is important in this regard to understand the fundamental perniciousness of social and environmental conditions such as racism, sexism, homophobia, and other forms of discrimination and injustice. In liberal intellectual communities there has at times been a tendency to romanticize the effects of such conditions as poverty and oppression through stories of heroes or heroines who have endured extremely difficult situations. It is certainly true that human beings are very resilient and able to survive great adversity. It is also true that some individuals have developed abilities in spite of highly unfavorable conditions. However, these individuals, like Horatio Alger in his economic success, are exceptions. Social dysfunction and mental illness are far more common among poor and oppressed populations than among the more fortunate. The reason that social inequality and injustice are wrong is that they create conditions that are severely damaging to the human capacity to create meaning.

7 Diagnostic Patterns in the Self

Since multiple factors from within the entire biopsychosocial spectrum will have had an influence on the current state of the self, it is not possible for a clinician to isolate and identify the specific cause of any client's problem. A good clinician will, of course, be alert to the possibility of etiological factors in fields in which social workers have no major expertise and will make referrals whenever appropriate. For this purpose a clinician must make a full assessment of the functioning of the client within the here-and-now interaction of the clinical contact as well as of the client's description of problems and goals in the current life situation. The assessment will indicate whether there are possible interventions into environmental conditions that might create a climate more favorable for the functioning of the client's capacity to create meaning. Such an assessment will also provide valuable information regarding the organization and derivation of the content of the client's meaning system.

Assessment, as understood here, is a broadly based picture of the person–situation configuration as this relates to the problem for which the client is being seen. Assessment would include, for example, information about physical status, economic resources, ethnicity, social class, education, past help-seeking behavior, and available social supports. Clinical diagnosis, as differentiated from assessment, is a much more narrowly focused evaluation of the client's capacity to create meaning. Diagnostic understanding is critical for the clinical social worker specifically because it provides guidelines for decision making in relation to the use of the relationship, the clinical social worker's primary intervention tool.

There has been such enormous confusion in the way pathology is categorized within the mental health field that it is often difficult to obtain consensus regarding the characterization of any given individual's problems. The major reason for this problem is, of course, the fact that there are so many disparate theoretical frameworks within which to identify the pathology, each calling attention to a different aspect of the client's functioning. The framework for diagnosis presented here utilizes a focus on the functioning of the self, reflected in the manner in which the client presents within the treatment setting. This framework, therefore, relies on an examination of the regulatory functioning of both the transitional and the operational selves and of the cognitive–affective structures utilized in the internalizing activity.

An understanding of the structures used in internalization in the diagnostic system described here owes much to the work of Katherine Nelson (1985). Since Nelson's work is relatively new, a brief introduction to her ideas might be useful. She has described meaning as having three different elements:

> First, it has been claimed that meaning is tripartite in nature and cannot be considered as a unitary concept. The evolved system consists of three parts: the cognitive representation of meaning, the communicative context of meaning, and the conventional meaning of words within the linguistic-cultural community. These three different ways of viewing meaning can also be seen as representing meaning for oneself, for one's communicative partners, and for the community at large. (p. 249)

In a well-functioning adult self all of these parts of meaning are used selectively, depending upon contextual requirements.

Chapter 5 described the initial structures within which the child builds the representational world as generalized event representations, that is, as scripts that have an ordered sequence of actions organized around a goal and appropriate to a particular spatiotemporal context. Since these event representations are abstracted from the world of the child's immediate experience, they contain culturally specific information. This information is obtained through interaction with the environment and is useful in communication with the human beings who also participate in the immediate cultural surround of the child.

The conceptual structures of meaning, in other words, the taxonomic categories that create classifications of items along lines of similarity, are formed out of the event representations. The aspect

utilized in the formation of abstract categories is initially determined by those characteristics that will appropriately fill a particular slot within a given event representation. Such categories are
later arranged in a hierarchy and linked to each other by notions of
causation. It is the conceptual level of meaning that contains the
individual's explanatory formulations of how the world works. The
conceptual level also contains the individual's abstractions about
his or her own identity and experience within the world. The
conceptual level is the one relied upon for the private meaning of
experience.

The lexical/semantic structure of meaning is used for communication with the community at large. At this level words are utilized
in accordance with their dictionary meaning and therefore are
communicatively useful in dealing with anyone familiar with the
linguistic code, that is, language, employed. The lexical/semantic
structures are the last ones developed, and their usage may influence the conceptual meanings of an individual's private experience. For example, the child who has derived pleasure from
sensual self-stimulation may experience this activity quite differently after acquiring the information from the broader community
that masturbation is naughty; a little girl may see herself differently after exposure to references to God as a male.

Although the semantic meaning of words may influence the
meaning experienced at the conceptual level, the words in the
lexical/semantic structure refer not to concepts but to other words
(as in dictionary definitions). For this reason the lexical/semantic
structure can be well utilized quite independently of any problems
within the usage of conceptual or event representational structures. In ordinary everyday interaction the conventional representations used in word meaning are at the semantic level; one
can talk quite easily about apple pie without accessing one's concept of "apple." Only when there are obvious disagreements
between people is it normally necessary for the disputants to com-
pare their private understandings of the concepts to which the
words refer.

Nelson's description of meaning as having these three parts is a
framework within which Basch's (1988) observation that there are
three different problems involving language usage that underlie
psychological pathology can be readily explained. According to
Basch, in *denial* perception is blocked so that the individual is
unable to utilize the information the stimulus might have contained. In *repression* the experience itself is registered but the
pathway to expression through language, either for the self or

others, is blocked; in repression language cannot be used to understand, organize, or communicate the experience. Finally, in *disavowal*, the pathway from linguistic symbols to the lived experience is blocked, so that the power of language to represent or recall the sensations of inner experience is limited.

Nelson's work is relatively new, and there is not yet a body of research linking her theory of language acquisition to functioning in adulthood. For this reason, the conceptualizations here must be considered tentative. Nevertheless, the conceptual fit between Nelson's formulations and preexisting observations about psychological pathology is so striking that it seems reasonable to think that a model utilizing these ideas could have considerable explanatory power.

Clinical experience indicates that in pathological functioning there is uneven development among the parts of meaning identified by Nelson, which are here referred to as structures. The individual with pathologic functioning, therefore, creates meaning in an established pattern that involves a differential overusage or underusage of the three structures. While there is an order in which the structures develop in childhood, it does not involve epigenetic stages; the structures do not supplant each other but function simultaneously. It appears that there is a considerable degree of resistance to regression built into the structures once they are established. In other words, in the adult the functioning of the transitional and operational selves is likely to be affected, either positively or negatively, by the conditions of the environment, but the structures used in internalizing are more stable. Under extremely negative conditions, however, the structures can also become eroded, and under prolonged positive conditions they can undergo further development.

Although the patterns of utilization of the structures of internalization do tend to be relatively stable in any given individual, the functioning of the transitional and operational selves responds to the conditions of the environment and this variation can also affect structure utilization at times. For this reason clinical diagnosis cannot be thought of as a one-time judgment. A clinician must be alert to the nuances of the meaning-making activity of the client at all times during the treatment encounter.

Any diagnosis should be based on the specific characteristics of the activities of the self in the particular individual. For purposes of illustration, this chapter will present case examples from diagnostic groups commonly encountered in practice and in the literature. These presentations are intended only for illustrative purposes.

Human functioning is so complex that no generalized system of diagnostic categories can capture the unique qualities of any individual. A diagnostic system, therefore, only provides a foundation upon which the clinician can elaborate in attempting to gain an understanding of the individual client.

The following outline indicates the description of ideal functioning according to the diagnostic criteria:

I. Transitional Self

1. A flexible interpsychic space is maintained through boundaries that modulate the degree of psychic closeness/distance in accordance with the perceived qualities of the environment.

2. Perceptual information is admitted at a relatively steady rate but one that is in accord with the state of energy available for internalization. Selective perception operates flexibly in accordance with the evaluative function of meaning, admitting information that is pertinent to the task at hand.

II. Operational Self

1. The level of energy devoted to internalizing activity varies in accordance with the level of physiologic energy available.

2. The level of energy devoted to internalizing activity also varies in accordance with the evaluation of the safety of the self within the current environment.

3. There is a high level of affect tolerance that is developed out of practicing the evaluation of the safety of the self in conjunction with positive experiences with human others who provide regulation and social referencing and that allows for regulative control over behavior.

4. There is a highly articulated experience of an inner life that has been developed out of practicing the evaluation of the safety of the self.

III. Structures of Internalizing Activity

1. There is a stable system of generalized event representations for use in communication with interacting partners.

2. There are conceptual forms of representation for use in inner thought.

3. There is lexical/semantic representation for use in communication with the broader linguistic community. The lexical/semantic structure can be used to capture representations at the conceptual and event-representational levels.

The charts and case illustrations presented in this chapter show some common pathologic patterns of meaning-making activity as they vary from the model of ideal functioning. They should not be considered to be representative of all possible problems in meaning-making activity.

As has been emphasized, diagnosis must be based on observations about the current state of the client, which may have been caused by many different variables. Scientific etiology cannot be established by the client's account of the history, since the objective accuracy of this story is highly unreliable. Nevertheless, the historical account is the content of the client's identity, and its relative coherence, differentiation, and integration as presented are important elements for consideration in understanding the functioning of the operational self and the relative development of the structures. Furthermore, the historical account provides the worker with a basis for empathic understanding. Finally, the client's historical account often provides clues as to possible bases for the patterns of meaning-making activity, even though these cannot be considered scientifically valid.

Clinical practice, including that of the medical profession, involves the construction of a narrative involving a plausible account of how the client/patient *might* have developed the presenting problem (Hunter, 1989). This constructed story, while not objectively scientific, is a type of hypothesis essential to the clinician in that it helps to guide the therapeutic interventions that will be utilized. One of the skills underlying good clinical practice is the ability to create an account of the client's history in which there is a relatively good fit between the client's presentation of the problem and the best available information from scientific research about etiological possibilities without significant distortions in either. In the diagnosis of the capacity to create meaning, the extent and manner of the client's participation in the creation of this story is also important information.

The clinician should be alert to whether there is a narrative fit between the client's account of his or her past and the clinician's understanding of environmental conditions that may have had etiological significance in the production of the current state of the self. In other words, it is useful in regard to a particular case example to examine the history presented by the client to know whether this presents a picture that is *consonant* with *possible causative factors*. One can feel more confident about the accuracy of a diagnosis of a particular pattern of meaning making in the self if the history provides a basis for understanding how such a pattern *might* have been instituted.

Four diagnostic patterns are presented in this discussion: psychotic functioning; character-disordered functioning; borderline functioning; and narcissistic functioning. Since it is not clear that neurosis is characterized by any one pattern, there is no pattern presented for neurotic functioning. It is likely that in neurosis the ability to utilize all three of the structures has developed but perhaps with some lack of integration between them. However, it is also true that individuals whose meaning systems have usually functioned well can be affected by adverse life events in a wide variety of ways and with no specific pattern resulting. This is in accord with Winnicott's (1956) idea that in neurosis adequate parenting has produced a healthy self and that neurosis is a tribute to the fact that life is difficult.

Psychotic Functioning

I. Transitional Self

1. Interpsychic space may be very open (leading to schizoid patterns) or very closed (leading to paranoid patterns), but there is little ability to make minor adjustments so that any boundary change is likely to be from one extreme to the other. Negatively experienced mergers are common.

2. The rate of admission of perceptual information varies, with very little admitted at some times and flooding at others. There is an inability to screen out information not relevant to the task at hand: All information is seen as having relevance for the safety of the self, a defect caused by major malfunctioning in the ability to construct evaluative meaning.

II. Operational Self

1. Coordination of the level of internalizing activity with the physiologic state may be difficult so that there may be periods of "racing thoughts" and periods of an almost vegetative state.

2. There is little ability to evaluate the relative safety of the self at more than a reflex-like level or to modulate internalizing activity in accordance with that evaluation. The expenditure of much energy in states presumed to be safe may lead to manic symptomatology; conversely, the withdrawal of energy under conditions of presumed crisis may lead to catatonic symptomatology.

3. Affect tolerance is very low so that, for example, even the presence or touch of another human being can be experienced as acutely painful. There is little regulative control over behavior.

4. Awareness of inner experiencing may be minimal or acute, but if acute it is apt to be extremely chaotic because of the ease with which the internalizing activity can become overloaded.

III. Structures of Internalizing Activity

1. There is difficulty in retaining stable event representations.

2. Conceptual representation is not well developed. Categories may not be abstracted from the event representations. The criteria by which any existing categories are formed may not be consistent or may include slot fillers that are inappropriate to the event representation. Thus, constructions regarding causality are apt to be limited or unusual, and thoughts appear to be peculiar.

3. The use of lexical/semantic representation may vary considerably, but it will have little relationship to the conceptual level of thinking, leading to the possible use of magical thinking—the notion that saying or thinking something can make it happen.

Case Illustration

Edith, an 18-year-old freshman, was brought to the infirmary of a large state university by her roommate during exam week of her first semester away from home at college. In an extremely agitated state, Edith paced the waiting room, mumbling incoherently something about cherry cobbler. Her roommate explained that Edith had been very worried about exams and had been studying late into the night for the past week. Edith had become extremely upset at dinner the night before and had since been pacing and claiming that she would be able to pass her examinations without studying because she was the Virgin Mary.

When seen alone, Edith became only slightly calmer but did manage to agree that she had been very worried about her ability to pass examinations. She claimed that she now knew she did not have to be worried because the fact that she had been given cherry cobbler rather than apple pie in the dinner line had confirmed that she was the Virgin Mary. She could provide factual data regarding her age, class, residence, and her family but could not provide a more satisfactory account of what had happened to her. She did agree that she was tired and would like to be able to get some sleep. The construction of an understanding of what had led up to Edith's acute breakdown required several months and the procurement of some information from interviews with her parents.

The oldest of four children, Edith had been conceived during her parents' high school romance. Both parents' families had been upset by the pregnancy partially because of the disparity between social status and ethnicity in the backgrounds. Her mother's family were Irish Catholic and worked in skilled-labor jobs. Her father came from one of the few Jewish families in the relatively small midwestern town. Her paternal grandfather, as the owner of a distributorship for farm machinery, was considered wealthy but was always insecure about his business since it depended on the goodwill and patronage of the gentile farmers. Thus, Edith's grandfather had always been hypervigilant about his family's public behavior and reputation in the town. Furious with his son over the illegitimate pregnancy, the grandfather had insisted upon marriage. Neither parent had felt there was much choice at the time, the father out of a pattern of habitual compliance and the mother because abortion was forbidden by religion.

Following the marriage, Edith's father worked in the family business, continuing his subservience to his critical father. When Edith's mother initially attempted to resist the grandfather's insistence that the couple adopt his own atheistic stance toward religion, she was horrified by her husband's terror of his father's disapproval. Edith's mother finally gave in to her husband's tearful pleading and complied, even though this gradually alienated her from her own family. However, privately she refused to utilize birth control, thereby beginning a kind of cold war between herself and her husband. The quiet hostility between the parents apparently fed on the father's unhappiness at work, where the grandfather continued to be critical, eventually promoting a favored younger brother to a higher position in the firm.

When Edith was 10, her grandfather died suddenly of a heart attack; her father's position at work improved little, with the brother having taken over running the business in accordance with the grandfather's will. After

Edith's grandfather's death, her mother surreptitiously reinitiated contact with her family, particularly her two sisters. Although officially the family continued to be atheistic and Edith and her three younger siblings were encouraged to make fun of religion, the mother frequently went to week-day masses with her sisters. Edith, who was forbidden to enter a church, was aware of and curious about her mother's family, about whom she knew little, and about her mother's apparent return to the faith. In her mind her mother's faith also became connected with the fact that her mother and her mother's two sisters were all called by their middle names, each having been given the first name Mary in accordance with a family tradition.

Edith's early relationship with her mother is not clear, although there is reason to believe it may have been affected by her mother's anger at the paternal grandfather's family rule. Edith became directly involved in the complicated family relationships at a very young age since the grand-father, apparently in an attempt to counteract any criticism by the towns-people of the forced marriage, frequently demanded that the mother and baby be lovingly exhibited at the business site. Once again Edith's mother had reluctantly complied.

As a youngster Edith had been a quiet, obedient child and a good student. She helped her mother in caring for the younger children and seemed to be close to a sister who was four years younger. For a time in grade school she had a best friend who lived nearby, and the two often played together, dressing their dolls and planning their own attire for school. But the friend moved away from town shortly after Edith's grand-father's death, and Edith seemed devastated by this. She remained socially isolated throughout high school, a good student but always feeling awk-ward around peers and having no dates. Edith was quite frightened of the idea of going away from home to college, but teachers had encouraged her in this regard and she had no idea what else she might do. She was actually surprised by her mother's enthusiasm for the idea of her having a future away from the town and by her usually distant father's agreement to foot the bills.

In the summer following graduation from high school, Edith landed a job working in the town library, a place where she felt relaxed and com-fortable. There she met Stan, a serious young man who was in his third year of agricultural studies and working on a nearby farm for the summer. He would come by the library in the evening, and the librarian, who thought the relationship cute, would sometimes leave them alone, allowing Edith to close the library. Usually when alone the two would simply talk about the books they were reading, but on one occasion Stan made an attempt to seduce Edith. Although frightened, Edith went along with some petting but began to resist strenuously at the possibility of actual intercourse, telling Stan that she had not done this before. She had not understood why he had gotten angry and, having had little exposure to sexual slang, did not understand what Stan meant when he yelled, "So keep your damn cherry" at her as he stormed out the door. This experience made her feel even more alone and frightened of what college might bring.

College turned out to be every bit as bad as Edith had feared. She had no idea how to make relationships with most of the other girls, who were constantly talking of dating and sex. Her roommate was pleasant but was an attractive and popular girl who frequently talked about men with other students who would visit the room. Edith desperately wanted to be alone but had a hard time finding ways of managing that. The library might have been a refuge, but there thoughts of her humiliation with Stan intruded. For the first time in her life she was having a hard time understanding her courses; terrified that she would not pass, she feared having to return home a total failure.

Edith did, however, make one friend: another quiet, shy, and very reserved girl who also seemed left out of the heterosexual activities and interests of most of the girls. Apart from classes, this girl's major interest was in religion. Initially reluctant, Edith began attending meetings of a Protestant youth group on campus with her friend and quickly became intrigued by the group and the religious rituals. Close to the end of the semester, the group, anticipating Christmas, held a meeting at which the "Cherry Tree Carol" was sung. The religious meaning of Christmas was still something mysterious to Edith, who later vaguely remembered hearing something in the song about Joseph being angry and Mary having cherries by command. A week later Edith, exhausted and overwhelmed by studying, went to the dining hall. As she reached the dessert counter in the cafeteria line the server apologized for having just run out of the apple pie that was on the menu and asked Edith if she would like some cherry cobbler instead. It was that night that Edith decided she was the Virgin Mary—after all, she had cherries by command.

In a state of acute psychosis Edith's meaning system has completely broken down. The transitional self is unable to modulate input, and in the resulting state of increased tension Edith is unlikely to be able to tolerate much interaction with others. Edith's operational self cannot, however, terminate the internalizing activity, and the excess energy evoked means that she remains in an exhausted state of hyperalertness. Furthermore, the internalizing activity is not in accord with her claims that she is safe from the threat of failure in her examinations; an observer might well have the impression that she does not believe her own evaluation.

In this state Edith's experience of her inner life is acutely experienced but very chaotic, and she is unlikely to have much ability to control her behavior. Human beings cannot generally tolerate such a state over an extended period of time. It is therefore likely that Edith will either return to a somewhat higher level of functioning or a chronic malfunction of the boundaries of the transitional self will be constituted. In the latter case, she would probably become either schizoid—that is, have boundaries that were chronically too open, leading to a state of depletion in the operational self—or paranoid, having too-closed boundaries, which would preserve the content of already constructed meaning but not allow for its alteration in accord with differing contexts.

Even in her state of acute confusion, Edith retains some of the lexical/semantic structure. There is, however, magical thinking in that she believes if she is referred to as the Virgin Mary, her potential failure will be averted. There is an underlying belief that all women with the name Mary are the same—a failure at the conceptual level to be able to form categories on the basis of single criteria while retaining a recognition that on the basis of other criteria these items differ. Even more basically, Edith suffers from a collapse of all three structures, as demonstrated by her understanding of the word, *cherry*. The word is part of the lexical/semantic structure, but she cannot utilize its different dictionary meanings; nor can she define it herself through the abstraction of some common element in all of the contexts in which she has encountered it. Instead, the word *cherry* comes to stand in a global fashion for the meanings of all her experiences with which it has been associated.

The difficulty that psychotic or near-psychotic individuals have in being able to build categories from event representations or to know the difference between slot fillers that are appropriate and those that are inappropriate can often be clinically observed. For example, a woman who was an experienced and excellent cook noted that she knew she was in danger of once again becoming psychotic when she found herself obsessing for hours; she had been trying to remember how much onion went into her recipe for chocolate chip cookies.

A clinician encountering Edith at the point of crisis would have no way of knowing for certain precisely how her transitional or operational selves had functioned earlier. However, her inability to recover sufficiently within a relatively short time to provide a therapist with a more coherent account of what had happened to her suggests the probable existence of some long-standing deficits.

The circumstances of Edith's birth into a family with unreconciled ethnic differences and with concerns about the prejudices of the community may have created an environment in which some interpsychic distance from others outside the family was encouraged. Within the family the father's anger apparently kept him at a psychological distance as well. Data from interviews with the parents suggest that mother may have been more available, at least in early childhood, but the interpsychic messages from mother may have been confusing, particularly at the times when she had to make a public show of her caring for Edith against her wishes. In addition, in this family there was apparently no open sharing of the meaning of perceptions about evaluatively important circumstances such as family participation and religion. Edith might, therefore, have had insufficient help in establishing competence in the development of conceptual structures.

It can be hypothesized that so long as Edith remained within the familiar context of her family, the capacity to create meaning that she did have was sufficient to enable at least minimal functioning. Her legitimate fear of how she would cope with college would have increased her need of soothing and social referencing. Since she felt comfortable in the library environment, the boundaries of her transitional self were more open there. Thus, Stan must initially have seemed like a welcome relief, more of a self-regulating other than members of her family and a provider of social referencing as well, through his sharing of information about survival at college. It is not known what Stan's behavior was about from his perspective, but for Edith at some point in their foreplay he became less soothing as a self-regulating other and more frightening even as he was expressing affection. It is at least possible that this may have recalled the early experience of being subjected to exhibitionistic but false displays of affection when at her grandfather's business site as an infant.

It is also very likely that the sexual impulses attendant to adolescence had also put a strain on Edith's functioning. Sexual feelings can, of course, be blocked from perception like any other, but since they are physically based they are more persistent. Incorporating sexual feelings within a comfortable individual and social meaning system is notoriously difficult for most adolescents and would normally be more so for an isolated youngster like Edith. At any rate, it is clear that Edith experienced the possibility of the fusion experience of sexual intercourse as a frightening and potentially disorganizing merger. For Edith the experience with Stan served, therefore, both to confirm her own inferiority and unacceptability to her peers and to signal the possibility of psychological fragmentation.

Edith's move to college placed her in a new environment, requiring the creation of significant new event representations, a task she apparently had trouble accomplishing. This difficulty was undoubtedly increased by her problems in screening out input when with her peers and by her problems in being able to be alone, or at least alone in a soothing environment. Thus, her capacity to create meaning began to function less well, and for the first time she was not able to deal with input in an academic environment, resulting in even more difficulty.

Character-Disordered Functioning

I. Transitional Self

1. Interpsychic space does not vary with the qualities of the environment but is kept at a constant, distant level. Closed boundaries mean there is little likelihood of merger experiences of any sort.

2. Perceptual information relating to the concrete external qualities of the environment is admitted at a relatively steady rate. Attention is not paid to information from affective communication, which is therefore denied.

II. Operational Self

1. The level of energy devoted to internalizing activity varies in accordance with the level of physiologic energy available. In general, however, more energy is likely to be devoted to physical action than to internalizing activity.

2. The level of internalizing activity varies in accordance with the perceived need to protect the safety of the self but is apt to be short-circuited by a quick resort to physical activity because of the fact that the ability to abstract an evaluation based on a representational world is impaired. The difficulty in achieving an evaluation of the self also leads to the expenditure of considerable energy in attempts at controlling the external environment.

3. There is little affect tolerance and little regulative control over behavior. Any increase in affect intensity is apt to trigger impulsive behavior.

4. There is little awareness of an inner life in the self or in others. Because of this, there is often a need for physical action in order to feel invigorated.

III. Structures of Internalizing Activity

1. Event representations are stable but rigidly retained. The construction of new event representations may require considerable effort.

2. There is a major deficit in conceptual forms of representation. The ability to form and utilize categories is limited to concrete perceptual information. The ability to arrange these categories within a hierarchical explanatory framework is also likely to be limited. Causal formulations are therefore based on concrete perceptual data and are viewed as totally correct or totally inaccurate.

3. There is considerable variation in the development of lexical/semantic representation, which may function well, but ability to access conceptual structures will be limited. Skill in the lexical/semantic arena will instead be used pragmatically to control the environment.

Case Illustration

Bob, a 25-year-old Caucasian of German–English descent, accompanied his 26-year-old wife, Alicia, to a Family Service agency where she requested marital counseling. Bob, recently discharged from the Marine Corps, complained that his wife was nagging him about getting a job and did not understand his need to relax while reorienting himself to civilian life. He was not sure he wanted the marriage but thought he would stay if Alicia could provide him with proof that her 4-year-old son, Jason, was his child. He believed that the fact that this request upset her so much meant that Jason was not his child.

Bob pointed out to both his wife and the social worker that he knew Alicia might try to lie to him about this but that he always knew when anyone did that. When still in high school, he said, he had loved the Sherlock Holmes mysteries. He still had a copy of the collected works of A. Conan Doyle, which was like his bible, and he had studied it enough to know how Holmes thought. So if Alicia would simply produce her proof, he could figure out if it were real or not. He wasn't sure what he would do if he determined she was lying but thought he might go back to the town where he was last stationed and look up a woman he knew there.

When seen alone in a separate appointment, Bob explained that he had returned to town after his discharge and was dismayed at finding Jason to be an unruly youngster with temper tantrums. He was convinced that Alicia had not been caring properly for the child and was not reassured by her assertions that Jason was upset by having his father become part of the household again. Bob thought it was not surprising that Jason should be so undisciplined since Alicia clearly did not run the household properly, as evidenced by her failure to have meals on a regular schedule.

An articulate young man, Bob related his history in a matter-of-fact manner. He had only one relative with whom he was in contact, a brother 3 years his senior who was married and living in another city. He thought he *might* have had a younger sister, but the child he remembered might just have been someone for whom his mother babysat. He was not sure what had happened to this child; perhaps she died. His mother had been an alcoholic, and Bob knew that in his early years the family had moved several times. His father, a construction worker, had tried to hold the family together and when Bob was 5 had left his wife, taking the boys to live with his mother. The grandmother was a strict woman who made the boys attend church, something Bob had not done before or since.

When Bob was 7, he and his brother returned to living with their parents, who had reconciled, but after a short time the mother returned to drinking. Bob remembered her taking him and his brother to a bar for dinner and his father coming to get them, often with a loud scene resulting. He pointed out that this was how he knew it was important for a child to have regular meals at home. When Bob was 10, his father left, severing contact with the family. A year later he and his brother went to live with a maternal aunt, since their mother was becoming ill from the alcohol. He saw little of his mother after that until he was taken to her funeral when he was 14.

Bob described his aunt as meaning well but having too many rules and being mostly concerned about her own children. When he was 16 he left school, where he was not doing well, although he saw himself as being very bright. After leaving school he worked in a couple of fast-food chains and hung around with a fast crowd. He indicated that at 18 there was a (unspecified) reason why it was "convenient" for him to "get out of town in a hurry," and he joined the Marines. Actually, he had originally wanted to join the Navy because he had heard that that branch of the service provided the best job training. But when he went to sign up, the Navy recruiter was not there and the Marine recruiter convinced him that Navy training would require more academic skill than he had. He had often regretted this, believing he would have been much more challenged in the Navy and maybe now would have more marketable job skills.

Actually, Bob had liked boot camp and had also done well in training for military guard duty. While stationed locally, he had met Alicia, who was working as a waitress in a restaurant/bar. Bob said he wanted to help her because she was trying to go to a community college as well as work and was having a hard time financially. He began spending his free time with her, living in her apartment when on passes and helping pay her bills. By the time she was pregnant, he already had orders to ship out. He had never been certain the baby was his or that Alicia might have had another boyfriend she saw when he was in camp, but he had married her anyway just so she would get an allotment check. He had not seen her or the boy much since then, coming back on leave only a few times.

Bob had decided to leave the Marine Corps as he was tired of being ordered around by men who did not know any more than he did. He thought that if he was going to be a civilian he ought to be responsible and take care of his son. However, he thought this would be pointless if, in fact, the boy was not really his son, which was why he wanted Alicia to give him some sort of proof. He thought she owed it to him after all the money she had gotten from his service benefits.

The major deficit in character-disordered individuals derives from an inability to abstract evaluative meaning about the safety of the self from event representations. As a result of this problem, the individual has only a globally experienced inner life, as well as difficulty in understanding the inner lives of others. This results in boundaries of the transitional self that react very little to the affective implications of environmental conditions. Since the individual has little basis for being able to understand interpersonal relationships, there is apt to be chronic suspiciousness regarding others. Bob, for example, sees himself as having given Alicia a great deal and has little understanding of how she feels about his request for proof of his paternity. With some character-disordered individuals, interpersonal relations can include callous exploitation.

Character-disordered individuals often have considerable difficulty constructing new event representations and using these as a basis for behavior. Not infrequently, this leads to devoting considerable effort to understanding the concrete elements of the external world and considerable pride in being "smart." Bob, for example, has adopted a strategy of looking for hidden clues in physical evidence, in the manner of Sherlock Holmes, in order to assure himself that he knows what is going on around him. This kind of awareness of the world is, of course, adaptive for some kinds of activities, though not for others. Bob does not know how to read affective communication from Alicia or from the social worker.

The lack of ability to abstract or evaluate experience results in inabilities both in learning from the past and in planning for the future in any consistent way. Meaning for the individual with character-disordered functioning remains embedded with the context of action and of the concrete external present. As Nelson (1985, 1986) has indicated, the child first learns to understand the world through event representations. Language and the advanced symbolic thinking that language supports is then superimposed on this foundation. It is therefore probable that the experience of a chaotic environment in childhood, one that makes it much more difficult for the youngster to create stable representations, may frequently be a significant etiological factor in pathology of this type. Certainly, Bob's early life sounds as if it might have been experienced as chaotic.

One of the reasons that the typical child can so readily construct event representations is that the child actively participates in the events captured in the early representations. Action, as Piaget (1962) suggested, precedes meaning in development. However, action alone is not enough:

> The essential claim here is that the child cannot get to language through action alone. Action must become represented on the cognitive level if it is to enter into the meaning system. In the present proposal, the level of event representations is the level at which actions, as well as people and objects, become represented. (Nelson, 1985, p. 253)

The construction of event representations, as has already been noted, is facilitated by experiences of soothing from a self-regulating other.

The functioning of adults with character disorders is consistent with the possibility that caretaking others may not have been experienced as self-regulating others, either in soothing or in exciting, at significant points in the individual's development. Perhaps more important, adults with character-disordered functioning may not have experienced caretakers as providing social referencing either. It is likely that the experience of consistent caring through the provision of social referencing from early significant others may be critical for the development of the ability to evaluate the safety of the self.

People with character disorders may have sufferred from emotional neglect. Individuals with this type of problem also tend to behave as if they have not yet fully comprehended the existence of a separate and independent mind in others, as if they had not fully formed Stern's (1985) domain of the intersubjective self. It is not merely that Bob does not understand Alicia; for him she is somewhat interchangeable with the woman he knew in the last town where he was stationed.

A deficit in the development of internal evaluative patterns of meaning leaves the individual highly dependent upon immediate cues from the external environment for a sense of safety and security and upon action for dealing with problems. Bob, for example, did not seek induction into the military until he was in difficulty of some type. Then he joined the branch of the service whose recruiter was available, in spite of a belief that another branch might have more to offer. Taking the future into serious consideration when making current decisions is not possible.

Conventional representation is not highly dependent on either reference or conception. Nelson pointed out that in the semantic use of language, which is language usage intended for the community at large, words are used to refer to other words rather than to things in the environment as in referential or conceptual usage. Thus, the person with character-disordered functioning is frequently highly articulate, with an ability to utilize language fluently. Yet the words, especially the words referring to feelings, have only weak and global connections to the inner states to which they purport to refer (Saari, 1976). Language is thereby utilized strictly for pragmatic purposes, for its ability to have an effect upon the environment.

Bob had apparently functioned fairly well in a military setting. This is typical of individuals with a character disorder who, although their impulsive behavior may create chaos in their lives, actually are more comfortable in a rigidly predictable environment, which is what Bob wants Alicia to create for him and for Jason as well. However, if a comfortable and predictable environment is achieved, there will be less external distraction from an inner life and more pressure for action because of a lack of affect tolerance. Thus, the individual is apt to be caught in a continual cycle in which impulsive actions cause undesired chaos.

Bob presented his history as if it consisted of objective facts and showed little feeling, with little modulation in the interpsychic space between himself and the social worker. He can use language well to describe things that are experienced as concrete/external and as a tool for attempts at controlling the environment, but its conscious meaning for his personal identity seems indistinct. It is important to note, however, that although it is questionable how much Bob is aware of the significance of his history, it has affected his behavior. It has become encoded in action patterns that are not a part of or accessible to him in a constructed meaning system. This is evident, for example, in his tendency to repeat behaviors that are similar to those of his father.

Borderline Functioning

I. Transitional Self

1. There are major fluctuations in the interpsychic space, with the boundaries making rapid shifts in the degree of psychic closeness or distance. These changes are in accord with the perceived qualities of the interpersonal environment, which also change frequently. The individual is at risk for merger experiences that are overwhelming and have negative effects on the capacity to create meaning.

2. There are major variations in the rate at which perceptual information is admitted. Information relative to the evaluation of the interpersonal environment is attended to closely while information about the concrete external world may be denied simply because including this information along with the many interpersonal perceptions would cause an overload for the internalizing activity.

II. Operational Self

1. The level of energy devoted to internalizing activity usually varies with the level of physiologic energy available but at times may be somewhat excessive or somewhat low, resulting in states of experienced anxiety and/or depletion.

2. The level of energy devoted to internalizing activity usually exceeds that which might be necessary for the safety of the self within the current environment. There is usually chronic hyperalertness lest the environment become threatening. The evaluation of the environment may shift in major ways in reaction to minor changes, particularly in the interpersonal environment. The rapid shifts in evaluation result

in large, rapid fluctuations in the need for internalizing activity, a condition to which the operational self ultimately adjusts usually through hyperalertness, but in some cases chronic exhaustion may lead to a state of oblivion.

3. The rapid shifts in the evaluation of the safety of the self result in much affect intensity from which considerable affect tolerance may develop. Nevertheless, there are apt to be difficulties in gaining regulative control over behavior because of excesses of experienced anxiety related to potential threats to safety.

4. There is usually much experience of inner life, but this is chaotic and is likely to be experienced in somewhat global, rather than differentiated and articulated, terms. In cases of exhaustion from the evaluative attempts, the experiencing of an inner life may become deadened.

III. Structures of Internalizing Activity

1. Generalized event representations are normally fairly stable.

2. There is an overuse of poorly formed abstract categories. There is difficulty in being able to retain consistency in the qualities utilized in abstracting these categories. Sometimes there is also difficulty in excluding slot fillers that are inappropriate to the event representation. The result is that the overall explanatory frameworks into which these concepts are integrated often seem unusual or peculiar.

3. There is not easy access between the lexical/semantic and the conceptual structures. Thus, the individual has difficulty putting lived experience into words (repression). Whatever skill in the lexical/semantic structure exists is used in an attempt at achieving some order in the conceptual structure. Conventional representation, therefore, is used with individualized definitions and often does not serve well in communication with the broader community.

Case Illustration

Margaret, a 43-year-old single black woman and mother of five children ranging in age from 9 to 28 years, sought treatment for the first time at a psychiatric clinic. Since she appeared in the waiting room wearing very casual clothes and moving to the rhythm of the music on her walkman, her social worker's first impression was of a very tough woman. Margaret started the interview by saying she did not know where to begin, then commenting, "My brain is a sponge. I can't take anymore." On welfare and living in public housing, Margaret had finished her GED about a year before and was now taking college courses to become a teacher but was afraid she might not be able to continue because of all her problems.

Margaret explained that she frequently has severe headaches when she wakes up in the morning. She has hypertension and has been on medication for this for 4 years, but her doctor suggested she seek additional help at the clinic since the headaches have gotten worse instead of better. Margaret said she wondered if they might be related to some of the bad dreams she frequently had at night. She had many different dreams, including one in which she is trying to get into a bathroom but cannot because there are no doorknobs. She commented that she sometimes wonders what she will find if she ever gets into the bathroom. Often the dreams are violent. Sometimes she can stop the violence while still dreaming by willing Roy Rogers to come and save her, but mostly she wakes up frightened and then has a hard time going back to sleep.

As Margaret talked of her problems, the social worker noticed that the toughness seemed to disappear and that Margaret was full of sadness and pain related to the events of her life. However, by the end of the interview, when Margaret was told that the intake worker might not become her regular worker, she became very angry and began questioning why she had needed to tell all this if she would only have to do it again.

The manner in which Margaret provided a history was extremely confusing. She began by talking about her father, attempting to tell the social worker everything about her relationship to him from birth to the present. She seemed to want to tell about her life moving from one relationship to another rather than along a time line, but the two frequently intruded on and confused each other. In addition, she would refer to someone newly introduced to her story by name and then assume the social worker knew all about her relationship to this person. Although it was possible for the worker to obtain an organized history, it was necessary to request clarifications frequently.

Margaret was the oldest of three siblings, born to tenant farmers in the southern part of the United States. She was an only child for a number of years and reported these as happy times. Her earliest memory was that of playing with dolls and having imaginary friends when she was 4 years old. A brother was born when she was 7 and then a sister when she was 9. She felt displaced by the siblings and marked the beginning of difficulties in her life with their births.

When Margaret was 10, her family left the South for a large northern city, the move being partially motivated by her mother's concern over the father's gambling and womanizing. The father's behavior in this regard only worsened in the North, however, and the family frequently had to move because of unpaid rent. By the time Margaret was 15 they were living in a public housing project; at that age she was gang-raped by three men. This resulted in her first pregnancy. Her parents did not believe she had been raped and encouraged her to keep the child, allowing her to remain in the home. However, after that, her father ignored her presence in the home. During this time Margaret met Dave, a man 14 years her senior, and began a relationship with him, becoming pregnant a second time when she was 17.

Margaret's father insisted that Margaret leave home after learning of the second pregnancy. Thereafter her relationship with her parents was somewhat distant. She moved in with Dave, with whom she then had a 22-year relationship and a total of four children. Dave consistently provided for the family financially but was often physically abusive. In the beginning Margaret did not fight back, but eventually she began to do so, which only increased Dave's violence. Finally, he stabbed her in the side, and she required 5 days of hospitalization. It was then that she began making plans to leave him, which she accomplished about 4 years ago. Even after she left him, however, Dave would find out where she was and assault her. He had not attacked her physically in some time but was still intruding into her life.

The major problems in Margaret's current life that brought her into therapy involved her children. Her oldest two children had left home and were doing all right with families of their own, but she still had three living with her, along with two young adult boarders. Her 17-year-old son had just been placed on probation for attempted sexual assault and her 13-year-old daughter had just become pregnant. She worried about what this was doing to her 9-year-old son. She indicated that things in the household were "out of control," with the children showing her no respect. It also hurt her that they showed so little concern for each other; they were "like strangers" to each other.

In contrast to character-disordered functioning, affect and the evaluative function of meaning are normally quite apparent at the borderline level of functioning. Margaret is highly sensitive to the meaning of the environment, and her boundaries reflect this. At the beginning of the interview Margaret's boundaries were closed. She used a Walkman and behavior suggesting exaggerated confidence in order to counteract her fear in the waiting room and the

criticism she may have expected at the clinic. When she sensed the
social worker's concern for her, Margaret's boundaries became
more open and she told her story with considerable feeling. Possible assignment to another social worker, however, brought anger
and a return to closed boundaries, which also helped her feel more
highly organized.

Margaret might well have described her problems in terms of the
behavior of others, economic stresses, or other problems that are
very real in her environment. Instead, she focused more on her
own inner life, telling the worker of her headaches and the dreams
that contain anxiety and sometimes violence. Margaret's problem
is not so much in the formation of event representations as in her
difficulty abstracting evaluative judgments about them, an effort
requiring much energy and attention. Although Margaret's metaphor of her brain as a sponge does not sound peculiar, it is not
unusual in working with individuals with borderline pathology to
discover that their problems in creating conceptual categories
mean that the metaphors are actually meant in a literal way. Thus,
Margaret might experience her headaches as evidence of her
brain's literally becoming too filled up, causing her fear of failing in
her school program.

The environment in which Margaret lives might well be judged
as chaotic by a detached observer. For many individuals with
borderline patterns of meaning-making activity, however, the environment is experienced as chaotic even if it seems quite tranquil to
an outside observer. This is because of the borderline person's
difficulty in being able to maintain a stable way of organizing
perceptions of the environment. Margaret, for example, had trouble sticking with the same organizing framework for her history.
This is a reflection not merely of poor communication skills but of
how she organizes and experiences her inner life. In addition, of
course, since Margaret is worried primarily about her headaches
and her inner life, she may simply fail at times to attend to some
aspects of her environment.

In contrast to individuals with character-disordered patterns of
meaning making, people with borderline characteristics are very
aware of affective communication and therefore can at times seem
very empathic. This is because they can achieve a conception of
what another person's inner life might be like and can appreciate
that inner chaos or difficulty can be painful. Individuals with borderline pathology, however, cannot usually sustain this conception
for very long or act consistently upon it because of the chaos of

their own inner experience. Thus, although Margaret's concern for her children, her sorrow that they are like strangers to each other, and her recognition that the household's chaos is a problem for them are all real, she is probably not able to institute and carry out a plan to behave in a way that might alter her children's experience.

Margaret seemed to relate well to the social worker's concern for her. Individuals with borderline patterns of meaning making do seem to have had experiences with soothing self-regulating others. However, frequently there are experiences with intrusive or abusive caretakers, so that the self-regulating other may be experienced as unpredictably alternating from soothing to pain-inducing. There is no way to know precisely how Margaret's early caretakers were experienced. However, her early history does not rule out an alternating pattern. On the other hand, her rape experience, her father's responses to her pregnancies, and the nature of her long-term love relationship suggest that she may have had caring/abusing relationships with men beginning in adolescence even if this did not exist earlier.

There is evidence in the literature that the ability to abstract conceptual categories out of event representations may be dependent upon the sharing of observations created out of event representations in interactions with other human beings. For example, Werner and Kaplan (1963) some years ago formulated a convincing theory that the ability to symbolize developed out of the sharing of perceptions of concrete objects with a significant other. Stern (1985) notes that the child learns through experiences of affect attunement which internal experiences can be shared. It is likely that the conceptual problems evident in the borderline individual are related to deficits in experiences of stable and affectively attuned interpersonal sharing.

Clinical evidence certainly suggests that individuals with borderline pathology have difficulty being able to communicate with others through the use of conventional language. There seems to be some difficulty in abstracting words from the personal aspects of the event representations in which they were learned so that they can be transcontextualized. One intelligent and educated woman, for example, thought the word moldy should be associated with bread and could not understand it as a metaphor for feelings (Saari, 1986). The lexical/semantic level of language has developed, but since it is experienced as not capable of capturing inner experience well, its ability to assist in the organization of experience is limited (Basch's idea of repression).

Narcissistic Functioning

I. Transitional Self

1. There is little variability in interpsychic space, with boundaries remaining partially open. There is little likelihood of merger experiences.

2. Perceptual information is admitted at a relatively steady rate that is normally in accord with the state of energy available for internalization. Information relative to both the concrete external world and affective communication is attended to, with the latter often attended to more closely.

II. Operational Self

1. The level of energy devoted to internalizing activity usually varies in accordance with the level of physiologic energy available.

2. There is an inability to evaluate information derived from affective communication. As a result, there are often attempts at obtaining information about the safety of the interpersonal environment from the admitted perceptions of the concrete external environment. Since an evaluation based primarily on such data is unreliable and difficult to achieve, there is a need for excessive energy in the internalizing activity, especially at times when some threat to safety seems possible. Evaluation of data about affective communication is often misinterpreted due to a failure to understand fully the experience of an inner life, either in the self or in others. The excessive energy spent on relatively small amounts of data often leads to a sense of depletion.

3. There is little affect tolerance, but there is more control over behavior than might be expected because there is also relatively little experienced inner life.

4. There is relatively little experienced inner life, with affective experiences often colored by a sense of unreality. There is a hunger for affectively meaningful experiences with human others that is usually not satisfied by actual interactions because of an inability to process this information. The difficulty in achieving reliable evaluations of the safety of the

interpersonal environment may lead to much experienced anxiety. There is often a generalized sense of a vaguely defined inability to deal with the problems of everyday living.

III. Structures of Internalizing Activity

1. Generalized event representations are normally fairly stable.

2. There are difficulties in conceptual structures, which are often not immediately apparent because of the overuse of the lexical/semantic structure. There may be underlying difficulties in being able to retain consistency in the qualities utilized in abstracting these categories or in excluding slot fillers that are inappropriate to the event representation. Frequently, however, the prominent difficulties are in being able to order these categories into hierarchically organized formulations about causal relationships in everyday events. In contrast to the expertise of the borderline individual, the expertise developed is more likely to involve categories of concrete, rather than abstract, items.

3. There is not an easy access between the lexical/semantic and the conceptual structures. The lexical/semantic structure is used as a substitute for the conceptual structure. Conventional representation, therefore, may be expertly used in communication with the broader community, but since it cannot access lived experience (disavowal), it does not serve well in relation to private personal experience. The overreliance on the lexical/semantic structure in relation to personal experience may also lead to some magical thinking in relation to the power of language, particularly in regard to an influence over other human beings.

Case Illustration

Nick, a 45-year-old divorced man of Italian descent who had several years of previous treatment, applied for psychotherapy with the main complaint being that his feelings got in the way of his being able to deal well with finances, with the result that he was not making enough money. The female social worker thought that Nick initially seemed a little frightened and perhaps somewhat depressed but that his confidence increased as the interview proceeded. Nick explained that he and his live-in girlfriend ran a computer consulting business together. He brought with him copies of several of his articles on computers, which had been published in business magazines, to demonstrate his expertise in this area. However, he admitted, his girlfriend makes about twice what he does in the firm and if he could solve his problems about money, it would "take a lot of the pressure off the relationship."

When asked to explain what he meant by his feelings getting in the way of his dealing with finances, Nick provided an example regarding his uncle's funeral. He had felt compelled to impress his relatives, so he bought an expensive three-piece suit and rented a Cadillac to attend the funeral. He realized that this was impulsive spending.

Nick described himself as the elder of two children. His father was a long-distance truck driver who was frequently away and was often a binge drinker when at home. His mother was a "manipulator" who was very involved in problems among her five siblings. She had not wanted children; she was hard of hearing and often used Nick as a sort of interpreter when he was a child. Nick believed he had not gotten along well with his peers in grade school because he was smarter than they were and they were jealous. However, in high school his grades had not been better than average, in spite of his superior intelligence, so the teachers had not permitted him to take the merit scholarship examinations, thus depriving him of money to attend college.

After high school Nick worked as a cabdriver for several years and married during that time. He and his wife did not want children. Gradually they grew apart. He thought this was because he had joined Mensa, had become more interested in using his mind, and had begun attending college. He thought his wife felt neglected because he was spending less time with her.

About a year after the divorce Nick began psychotherapy, which lasted for about 4 years. His therapist was a man who Nick thought had helped him become more interested in women who would not reject him. Nick explained that at this time in his life he had slept with over 100 women, most of whom he met through a singles club of which he was the president. The therapy had eventually come to "an impasse," and Nick stopped going. He acknowledged that he still owed the therapist money for unpaid sessions. Several years later Nick sought therapy again, this time from a woman who, he knew, had been a student of his previous therapist's. This did not work, however, since Nick felt he knew more than she did and did not want to waste his time teaching her.

When asked what he thought he needed from therapy this time, Nick said he wanted someone who could understand him well enough to use "accurate empathy" and embarked on a monologue full of psychiatric jargon about the importance of transference. He indicated that this time he would need a male therapist because his current girlfriend would be jealous of a female therapist.

It is not unusual for people with narcissistic patterns in meaning making activity to seem pleasant and healthy in initial or superficial social contacts. These people can utilize conventional language well and seem very invested in interaction with other human beings. Indeed, they normally are quite hungry for affectively meaningful human relationships. This hunger leads to behavior that seems to seek admiration from others, but once attained, the admiration is not experienced as satisfying because it cannot be used to help in the organization of the internal world of personal meaning. Others who engage in a relationship with such an individual often find that the relationship seems not to develop any more intimacy than was present from the outset.

Individuals with narcissistic disorders have problems in the relationship between the conceptual aspect of meaning and the lexical/semantic one, the reverse of the situation with borderline functioning. Whereas in borderline functioning the person will attend to inner experience and then not be able to capture that experience in words, the individual with a narcissistic pattern shows a heavy reliance on the use of language in a lexical/semantic sense but then cannot relate these words well to an inner experience. Basch referred to this as disavowal. Individuals with narcissistic problems both overvalue the spoken word and have an intuitive understanding that their own words are somewhat meaningless because they do not refer to an inner state. Therefore, the much sought admiration of others is inevitably experienced as empty as well.

Individuals with narcissistic patterns of meaning making have the same range of deficits at the conceptual level as do borderlines, but because they can utilize semantic language so well the problems are often not nearly as apparent in everyday functioning. The narcissistic pattern of language use functions like Winnicott's (1960) hypothesized "false self," protecting the individual from the experience of inner disorganization that can result from problems in the conceptual structure. It is at the conceptual level that the meaning of the experience of interaction with others must be comprehended, and affective communication with others is precisely what persons with narcissistic disorders cannot process. Nevertheless, they frequently will devote much energy in attempts at processing this information.

Individuals with narcissistic functioning often have little awareness of their own feelings or those of others. As one woman remarked while in treatment, "I really have no idea what makes
other people do what they do." The narcissistic lack of empathy for
others is often noted in the literature, sometimes with critical or
almost punitive overtones. What is often not highlighted is how
incredibly handicapped those who must live in a social environment are if they cannot understand affective experience and affective communication. Yet, because of the facility with language
characteristic of individuals with narcissistic pathology, it is easy
for associates—and, indeed, often even for therapists—to miss the
severity of underlying problems, which typically are in the areas of
self-satisfaction, self-esteem, and intimate relationships.

Individuals with narcissistic problems, with their intuitive knowledge of the emptiness of words, frequently acquire numerous
material possessions as presumably more reliable signs of well-
being and in an attempt to understand the interpersonal messages
that might be hidden in the concrete external aspects of the environment. These pursuits often require considerable energy, which
provides little payoff in the long run, and usually simply distract
the individual from more productive activities. Not infrequently,
the person with a narcissistic pattern becomes depressed around
midlife, by which time it has become painfully clear that existing
life achievements are providing little inner satisfaction.

Nick characteristically sought admiration from the female social
worker by showing her the articles he had written, by displaying
his knowledge of the therapeutic process, and by stressing his
sexual prowess with women. He presented his problem as one in
which feelings get in the way making money, yet the example he
provided related not to making but to spending money. He related
neither his feelings about his uncle's death nor his relationship to
him. Similarly, although there was an implication that the financial
problem was creating difficulties in his relationship with his girlfriend, he did not describe her or her feelings.

It is important to note not just Nick's lack of awareness of
feelings but also the global quality of his ideas about causation.
Making more money, Nick believed, would somehow improve his
relationship with his girlfriend, but it is not clear that Nick understood the relationship between the two. Conceptual difficulties in
formulating notions of why people behave as they do often leave
those with narcissistic problems with a sense of powerlessness in
regard to the world around them, as well as a belief that others are
just somehow luckier than they in life. Deficits in the ability to

comprehend interpersonal causation, combined with the overreliance on the lexical/semantic structure, also lead to magical thinking in the form of a belief that words can make things happen. Therefore, as is the case with Nick, there is often an overreliance on a therapist's words and a tendency to overvalue therapeutic jargon.

Like persons with borderline pathology, narcissistically disturbed individuals seem to have had soothing experiences with self-regulating others, since they know to seek out such relationships. It is possible that, at least in some cases, the deficit in the area of causal formulations might have resulted from a lack of adequate social referencing from the self-regulating others. In general, however, clinical experience with narcissistic pathology suggests that the individuals involved have a history of significant others who used them exploitively as self-regulating others, rather than providing such regulation; in other words, the regulation provided was in tune with the caretaker's needs rather than the child's. Nick's history, for example, includes a mother who did not want him but who used him to help make up for her hearing deficit. His performing as an interpreter for his mother, of course, may also explain some of his developed overreliance on lexical/semantic structures.

8 Therapeutic Use of the Self

There has been a long-standing debate among psychodynamic theoreticians as to whether the curative element in treatment is cognitive insight or the affective quality of the relationship with the therapist. As Stolorow (1988) has pointed out, this debate began with Freud, who in his last works seemed to be saying that a positive transference to the analyst is most important. Stolorow, however, also noted that from the perspective of current theory this debate is based on the false premise that human subjectivity can be divided into affect and cognition. Stolorow proposed that psychoanalysis is really concerned with meaning, which is an indivisible amalgam of affect and cognition, a position that is certainly endorsed here.

In another sense, however, the traditional debate can be seen to involve the issue of whether the therapist's use of content or of self in treatment interactions is more primary. From the perspective of the current work all therapy involves both content and the use of self in ways that are simultaneous and highly interrelated. The general question of which is more important seems unanswerable, since in work with some individuals content may be more important whereas with others the use of self may be. Interestingly, if transference is understood as being meaning, which Loewald (1960) proposed, then Freud's positive transference would actually involve both content and the use of self.

In spite of the fact that content and the use of the self in treatment can only be separated conceptually, at present an increased understanding of clinical social work treatment can be achieved through making a distinction between these two elements in examining their therapeutic effects. This separation is being made not in order to lay the foundation for a pronouncement regarding which is more effective but, rather, to clarify the role played by each and to examine their fundamental interrelatedness. The therapeutic use of the self is considered in this chapter, and the therapist's use of content is the focus of Part III.

Treatment involves an interpersonal interaction that is purposeful and goal directed. Clients normally approach therapy with ideas regarding how they would like their lives to change; if treatment is to work, it must be primarily directed toward a facilitation of client aspirations. The goal toward which the treatment is directed, however, needs to be based on a negotiated agreement between the client and the therapist that takes into account both client aspirations and the expertise of the therapist. The primary expertise of a clinical social worker is in using a relationship to help the client participate more effectively in culture through the modification, maintenance, or further development of the capacity to create meaning.

A relationship is more than a simple interpersonal interaction and is essential to treatment. One can, for example, buy goods at a store perfectly well without having a relationship with the clerk, but clinical social work cannot occur without an exchange of information and a shared attempt at understanding the meaning of that information. Indeed, the human creation of meaning can occur only within the context of an interpersonal relationship. The client–therapist relationship will inevitably come to have importance to the client, since it is the means to achieving the client's goals. It is within the context of the client–therapist relationship that the client practices and refines the skills in the creation of meaning that he or she will ultimately use in interpersonal interactions outside the treatment context.

Differential Use of Treatment Formats

There are now a number of treatment approaches and modalities that have been described in the clinical literature. These include not only individual, couple, family, and group modalities but an almost infinite number of combinations of such modalities with special techniques that may or may not be derived directly from theories. Often practitioners will espouse a particular methodology and attempt to become expert in that arena. At times there are even claims for the superiority of one approach over all others that may be available.

There has been sufficient experience with various treatment modalities to indicate that a wide range of intervention approaches can be effective. There is no evidence that any one modality is superior to all others. Rather, the expert practitioner needs to be able to fit the modality utilized to the particular client–situation configuration in question. While individual clinicians and agencies frequently make judgments about how best to plan such fits, there is remarkably little in the literature about this problem.

Loewald (1960) indicated that treatment provides the patient with a new environment that offers the opportunity for new and renewed growth. The therapeutic environment, however, should be one that is created specifically to provide the features that the client as an individual appears to need for that resumption of growth. The context in which treatment takes place—including the setting and the role prescriptions, whether the latter are formalized or not—has a major influence on how an interaction with a clinician is experienced. When therapy is considered to involve the creation of meaning, this significance is even more obvious, since the interpretation of meaning is always context-dependent.

The treatment context actually includes both a social structure and a culture. The social structure includes such things as rules for confidentiality, meeting schedules, and fees, but it also includes rules that govern participation such as who is to set the discussion agenda, how respect is to be shown, and how disagreements are to be handled. The authority of the clinician, presumably derived from that person's professional expertise, normally allows that person to set the social structure for the treatment enterprise. It may often be necessary for the structure utilized to afford individuals an opportunity for more active and egalitarian social participation than they have experienced in the past. The culture of any particular treatment, which refers to the meaning of the interactions within the social structure, will be mutually created by the social worker and the client. As is the case in any context, the nature of the social structure will have a significant influence on the character of the social interactions that take place within it and on the content of the culture that is created.

Bruner has noted that even prior to the child's use of speech there are routinized interactions with the caretaker in which each participant knows what to expect from the other. For the infant these interactions are common and may be obvious in tickling routines or playing at bath time. Bruner (1983) has called these routines "formats" and defines them as follows:

A format is a contingent interaction between at least two acting parties, contingent in the sense that the responses of *each* member can be shown to be dependent on a prior response of the *other*. Each member of the minimal pair has a goal and a set of means for its attainment. Each has the capacity to affect the other's progress toward their respective goals. The goals of the two participants need not be the same; all that is required is that the conditions of communal response contingency be fulfilled. (p. 132)

Bruner indicates that formats "grow" in the sense that they become more varied and complex. They serve as the basis from which the child ultimately learns to utilize symbols and becomes "socialized." The therapeutic environment can be understood to be an extended format in Bruner's sense.

Bruner's conception of meaning and language acquisition is that these develop out of the context of social interactions. When applied to the treatment situation, Bruner's formulation would appear to indicate that the social interactions that occur in the therapy setting provide the foundation out of which the meaning that is created there will grow. This idea is, of course, at considerable variance with the rationale behind the social structure Freud designed for analysis. Believing that meaning preceded action, Freud attempted to limit the patient's opportunities for action within the treatment setting so that the underlying meaning could emerge.

Although clinical social workers and other psychotherapists may not specifically utilize the couch or other Freudian techniques, there has until relatively recently been a tendency to accept the idea that the treatment setting designed by Freud is the ideal, to be modified only to whatever extent was essential if the patient could not utilize it. In fact, this can almost be thought of as using the couch as a Procrustean bed. A theoretical exploration of the manner in which the format for treatment affects the relationship and the capacity to create meaning, as this varies in different clients, is long overdue.

To date, Langs's (1979) position regarding the need for the rigid maintenance of a constant environment in treatment has been quite influential. According to Langs, the therapist's activity with the patient should be confined to verbal interpretation and this should occur only when both the patient and the therapist are seated in their proper and customary positions within the treatment room. Langs believed that any modification of this and other prescribed rules is a violation of the frame and essentially a therapeutic error. Most therapists regard Langs's position as somewhat extreme, and there has been some criticism of it, with Siegelman (1990, p. 148) even referring to it as inhumane. However, the goals of maintaining constancy in the treatment setting and of relying heavily on the use of verbal interpretation do have a general acceptance in many clinical circles.

The question may then be asked, What type of client would be likely to benefit from an experience utilizing this traditionally designed format? Clients with borderline patterns of meaning making have particular needs for the therapist to behave in a consistent and predictable manner in order to help achieve some stability in the functioning of the transitional self. In addition, these clients, who are in touch with a chaotic inner life, can utilize connections between affects experienced in the conceptual structure and words from the lexical/semantic structure to achieve greater organization.

The traditionally prescribed format for therapy, therefore, can be seen to have usefulness for clients with borderline symptomatology. The psychotherapy literature has generally been dominated by descriptions of individuals with borderline patterns of the self. It is therefore quite possible that therapists who stick rigidly to a frame have success primarily with clients with these problems. It is also possible that because of the tendency toward criticism of treatment in which there is a "violation of the frame," successful endeavors that do not conform to this presumed standard may not be as likely to be described in the literature.

While individuals with borderline patterns of the self may be able to use lexical/semantic structure to help organize their inner lives, a reliance purely on verbal interpretations is not likely to have especially beneficial effects on individuals with narcissistic patterns who use disavowal. In fact, since for these clients words have weak connections to a world of personal meaning, a heavy reliance on language may merely cause the entrenchment of their established pathology. In these cases it may instead be indicated for the therapist to be much more interactive, particularly by being alert to nonverbal affective communication and to possibilities for nonintrusive interventions that the client can interpret as evidence of empathic sharing on the part of the therapist. Helping the more narcissistically inclined client connect such acts to words may also be helpful. The existing literature on the treatment of narcissism does, of course, emphasize the importance of empathy.

In work with one severely narcissistic man it proved useful for the client and the therapist to drink coffee during the sessions. The preparation of the coffee with the correct amount of cream and sugar for each person became a kind of ritual, perhaps like a Japanese tea ceremony, that served as a nonverbal way of affirming mutual caretaking and a social interrelatedness. This simple physical interaction, first initiated by the client, became stylized in the sense of Bruner's formats. Furthermore, once the standards for the ritual had been established, small deviations from the client's usual practices could be seen as communications regarding his current state of mind. It therefore became possible to use this ritual to help the client become more involved in affective communication, which in his case was essential for the further development of the capacity to create meaning.

Current theories about the development of the capacity to create meaning emphasize the need for social participation. Nelson(1985) stresses the following in her conception of development:

> This view of early development has two emphases that distinguish it from otherwise similar views. First, it emphasizes the essential role of the development of conceptual representation independent of but interactive with language development. Second, it emphasizes the child's *participation* in events as the source of conceptual knowledge rather than simply the child as agent of instrumental action. *Participatory interaction* is seen as essential to the child's acquisition of meaning, not only because language is used within interactive contexts but because these contexts provide the structures that make mutual interpretation possible; structures of action, causality, contingency, reciprocity, and role-taking are essential to understanding the meanings encoded in language. Without the social interactive basis for conceptualization, the child's meanings would be confined to concepts of small objects, and both language and thought as we know it would be thereby impossible. (p. 253)

Interactions with clients need to be goal-directed and guided by professional ethics, but current theory indicates that clinicians who do not allow for any mutual social participation and who merely offers themselves as a blank screen are not likely to be effective. The format for interaction with a client does need to be geared to the diagnostic understanding of the client's capacity to create meaning. Therefore, for example, borderline clients may need more of a structured constancy while those with narcissistic pathology will need more active and affective interaction.

Nelson's ideas about the need for the child to participate in social interaction take on an added significance in considering treatment with people with character disordered or psychotic pathology. For these individuals major attention has to be given to the formation and retention of stable event representations that can serve as the basis for conceptual development. Since there is a likelihood that in both patterns some experienced environmental chaos has contributed to the development of the problems, a stable and predictable social structure would seem indicated.

Within a predictable social structure, however, the individual with character disordered or psychotic patterns of the self may need considerable experience in active participation in social interaction coupled with attempts at formulating affective meaning related to these interactions. For character-disordered and psychotic individuals, therefore, involvement in treatment formats (such as group, milieu, or family therapy) that can offer a wider range of interactive possibilities is often indicated, although a combination of family or group treatment and individual therapy may be ideal.

Individuals with character-disordered patterns of meaning making have some established event representations, but these are not established sufficiently well to serve as a basis of evaluative activity or to allow for modification through experience in social interactions. Such individuals often need controlled and affectively examined experiences in social interaction in order to modify closed boundaries in the transitional self, to make even small increases in affect tolerance, and to attempt internally based evaluative assessments. It is not surprising, then, that some of the most successful treatment with these individuals has utilized family, group, or residential treatment formats. The successes of self-help groups such as Alcoholics Anonymous or Adult Children of Alcoholics with this population becomes more understandable.

Family, group, and residential formats also provide more opportunity for the individual client to participate in activities aimed at evaluating and modifying the social structure of the treatment enterprise (Rubenstein & Lasswell, 1966). For many severely mentally ill individuals the opportunity to participate in a social structure where there is a less depreciating culture than may be encountered in the broader society and where it is possible to have effectance experiences (White, 1963) may be critical to stimulating growth in the capacity to create meaning. Conversely, if such formats are utilized in a manner that does not encourage participation but merely demands social compliance, the meaning making capacity is likely to become further eroded. Social participation in these formats should simultaneously facilitate the formation of stable event representations.

It is very likely that if clinical social workers can gain more understanding of the manner in which the differential use of treatment formats affects the individual's capacity to create meaning, far more creative ways than have yet been imagined of using the therapeutic environment and the self within it can be invented.

Managing Interpsychic Space

The idea of empathic relating on the part of the therapist has been basic to all theories of clinical work. Yet specific definitions of just what empathy entails have been elusive (Lichtenberg, Bornstein, & Silver, 1984). Part of the difficulty here is that clinical empathy has at times been thought of as some internal quality that is either inherent in the personal qualities of the therapist or can be achieved through experience and training and then applied to all clients. Empathy is more usefully considered to be an active way of relating in which the clinician stays attuned to the state of the client's self and then uses his or her self differentially to create an interactive context that maximizes the client's ability to function.

This differential use of the self, then, must always be based on a careful tracking of the current state of the client's self, which may vary from moment to moment within any given interaction. It is for this reason that it is never possible for an outside consultant to provide a prescription for how a clinician should specifically interact with a client. A consultant can only hope to help the clinician understand diagnostic patterns and the principles of attunement that can be utilized.

There are so many different variables that affect the client's state that it hardly seems surprising that even the most experienced and talented clinicians often find that in retrospect some of their interactions were less than perfectly empathic. Perfect attunement is not, of course, necessary for good treatment. It is, however, important for the clinician to make whatever adjustments are necessary to allow the client's self to function at the maximum capacity possible and to avoid fragmentation from overload or merger. A client will, of course, normally attempt to modulate the interactive distance in accordance with his or her needs.

There are a number of ways individuals attempt to control interpsychic space. These are used by all human beings in their interactions with each other. The difference in therapy is that the clinician learns to use these in a purposeful and disciplined manner. Love decreases interpsychic distance while hate increases it (Blanck & Blanck, 1977). Thus, expressions of concern ask for more intimacy whereas anger and criticism are requests for less intimacy. Awareness of Stern's vitality affects and of attunement through these is important for a clinician, since these can be used interpersonally either to engage or to disengage. Impersonal content, such as discussions about the weather, can be used to create more distance whereas discussions about highly personal topics such as sexual intimacy or areas that are known to be affectively charged for the individual will decrease interpsychic space. A familiar and predictable environment or one that is experienced as safe will allow the individual to permit more open interpersonal boundaries.

Knowing that there is a relationship between the pace at which internalizing activity can operate and the degree of interpsychic space, the clinician can utilize his or her interventions to assist the client in maintaining an appropriate balance between these two activities. It is important to understand that this definitely does not mean that the clinician should always simply express care or concern. These serve as invitations to increased closeness, and there are times when what a client needs most is some interpsychic distance in order to process perceptions, but may nevertheless need to do this in the presence of another person. Additionally, if a client begins to experience a threatened overload, he or she may need to utilize anger in order to close boundaries temporarily and to increase the sense of organization of the inner life. When this occurs, the social worker generally needs to allow the anger without responding defensively to it and to step back until such time as the client is ready to permit a closer engagement.

In the short run, the clinician generally needs to respect the messages signaled by the client about the currently desirable degree of interpsychic space and to respond accordingly. It is then necessary to evaluate the effect of any changes in the use of the self on the client; Schwaber (1981) has described this as the therapist's listening for the effect of the context on the patient. This short-run attunement should contribute to the longer-range goal of increasing the client's capacity to create meaning, with its accompanying results of increased affect tolerance and a more articulated but integrated experience of inner life.

The direction in which the clinician will wish to modify the interpsychic space in the long run depends, of course, on the diagnostic pattern of meaning making used by the client. In work with an acutely psychotic individual it may be important simply to establish the possibility of a relatively stable space that can be tolerated by the client even if only for brief periods of time. Clients with borderline pathology are often challenging in that the therapist must track and respond to the frequent shifts in interpsychic space with gradual attempts at reducing the extremes involved. In work with people with character disorders a major long-term goal is to decrease the degree of interpsychic space.

Factors Influencing the Current State of the Self

Many different factors can influence the current state of the client's self. The activity within the transitional and operational selves of an individual at any given time can be seen to reflect (1) the level of physiologic energy available in the organism for use in the creation of meaning; (2) the individual's affective-cognitive evaluation of the current state of the self; (3) the influence of the environment as currently evaluated by the person; (4) the effects of past experiences on the individual's level of ability to construct a representational world through internalizing ability; (5) the specific content of the already constructed representational world, including any expectations for the future; and (6) the relative match between the content of the person's representational world and the content of the current cultural surround.

Available Level of Physiologic Energy

Of the six factors affecting the activity of the self the level of physiologic energy available in the organism for use in the creation of meaning requires perhaps the least elaboration here. On the one hand, it seems fairly obvious that the clinician needs to be alert to conditions involving physical health. Encouraging major participation in the creation of meaning from a client who is ill may compound problems through a decrease either in available energy for physical functioning or in self-esteem, which can result from a failure experience. Yet the effects of physical illness or neglect of good health care may at times be very subtle. A full discussion of such effects is, however, beyond the scope of this work. At present, therefore, the statement that the clinical social worker needs to be aware of possible effects from a wide range of diseases—from alcoholism and AIDS to such things as hypothyroidism and diabetes—will have to suffice. Clearly, medical consultation is essential in some cases.

Current State of the Self

The individual's affective–cognitive evaluation of the current state of the self may be indicated to the clinician through a direct verbal statement about a feeling state like invigorated or disorganized. Usually, however, such a state is more indirectly communicated through client-initiated attempts at a shift in interpsychic space. It is important for the clinician to be aware that shifts toward increased space may signal any of several different possibilities: (1) there is a threat of a negative merger from too much closeness; (2) the operational self is reacting to an overload of input that cannot immediately be processed by the internalizing activity; or (3) the meaning of communicative content is threatening self-esteem or perceived safety. It is usually best for the clinician to respond to the indicated need of the client and then attempt to understand what motivated the shift. Whether or not to share with the client an awareness of the change in interpsychic space or a curiosity about its motivation is a further judgment that depends on how much the client can tolerate intimacy at the time.

Evaluation of the Environment

The influence of the environment as currently evaluated by the person is an area that is often neglected by psychoanalytic writers who tend to assume that the patient has already determined that treatment is a positive and desirable thing. Clinical social workers, especially those in host settings like hospitals, schools, or correctional facilities—as well as those who work with children—cannot make such assumptions. Through the social status and cultural meanings attached to the host setting, the environment beyond the clinician's office may significantly affect the client's understanding of the meaning of the therapeutic encounter. This meaning may then affect both the interpsychic space and the client's ability to devote energy to meaning-making activity. For this reason it is important for clinicians to understand what meanings about therapy clients may bring with them and to devote considerable effort in host settings to ensuring that clients are treated with respect in all contacts within the setting, since the meanings the setting holds for clients have direct effects on clients' ability to utilize services.

It is important that constrictions in meaning-making activity based on a negative evaluation of the meaning of therapy not be mistaken for more persistent deficits. The wish not to engage in therapy, or not to do so at any given time, is not necessarily

evidence of pathology. Gentle attempts at helping a client understand the reasons for and purposes of treatment often can help to
soften negative evaluations. Many clients may, of course, retain
some ambivalence about therapy even though overtly agreeing to
engage in it. When the negative side of such ambivalence is trig-
gered, this can cause an increase in interpsychic space and a
decrease in meaning-making activity at any time in treatment.
When this occurs, of course, the clinician will need to respond
facilitatively by allowing the client whatever temporary interpsychic distance is needed while helping the client retain some sense
of relatedness.

Although clients often feel reassured by the knowledge that the
clinician is an expert who can take charge of the treatment, they
may also feel threatened by the possibility of negative evaluative
meaning in the clinician's comments or by a meaning-making pace
that demands too much change from them. It is for this reason that
it is wisest to offer specific interpretative comments only when the
client seems ready for them and to offer them not as established
facts but as tentative speculations that the client can either accept,
reject, or modify. Bollas (1983) commented on Winnicott's technique in this regard:

> Any examination of Winnicott's clinical case presentations will illus-
> trate a person who certainly worked in a highly idiomatic way, and
> yet he concerns himself in his clinical theory with the unintrusive
> function of the analyst, with the analyst as a facilitating environment.
> How is it possible to be so idiomatic in one's presentation of interpre-
> tations and not be traumatic to the patient? In my view, the answer
> lies in the way Winnicott regarded his own thoughts; they were to him
> subjective objects, and he put them to the patient as objects between
> patient and analyst rather than as official psychoanalytic decodings
> of the person's unconscious life. (p. 7)

The Ability to Construct a Representational World

The effects of past experiences on the individual's level of ability to
construct a representational world through internalization have a
major effect on the activities of the individual's transitional and
operational selves as seen in treatment. Although events of the past
cannot be definitively ascertained, there is often a correspondence
between the manner in which clients behave in treatment and the
history they report. For example, a woman with such severely
borderline pathology that she was almost psychotic complained of

constant sexual abuse by her father. In the treatment hours she anxiously paced, showed difficulty in remaining with the therapist at times, and indicated that sometimes "the then becomes the now" so that whomever she was with seemed to become her father. Clearly, intervention in such a case calls for the clinician to utilize the self to maximize the experience of a soothing self-regulating other while minimizing intrusiveness. More ambitious attempts at altering meaning in this type of situation are likely to be counter-productive.

The Content of the Representational World

A discussion of the manner in which the clinician understands the specific content of the already constructed representational world, including any expectations for the future, occurs in Part III, which focuses on identity. It is nevertheless important to point out here that the content of the client's constructed meaning can influence his or her relative need for interpsychic space and his or her ability to devote energy to meaning making activity. Therefore, this factor must also be taken into account in the therapist's use of self in attempts at maximizing the client's ability to function. A negative self-image, for example, may affect the level of energy available for the creation of new meaning in addition to creating a need for interpsychic distance due to expectations of criticism.

Current Cultural Surround

Since a mismatch between the preconstructed content of the meaning system and the perceptions of the current environment can greatly increase the need for new meaning and strain the functioning of the internalizing activity, the relative match be-tween the content of the person's representational world and the content of the current cultural surround is another factor that can influence the client's need for interpsychic space within the treat-ment situation. When an individual has recently moved from one culture or environment to another, a mismatch between them is apt to be a major factor in his or her functioning. Similarly, the clinician needs to be alert to the possibility of negative effects on the client's ability to create meaning when there are significant cultural differences in the social worker–client match.

There are, however, more subtle ways in which differences be-tween the content of a representational world and the cultural surround can affect clients. The treatment enterprise itself has a kind of culture associated with it. Frequently, there is a tendency on the part of clinicians to assume that clients know much more than they actually do regarding role expectations during therapy. At least in the beginning of a contact many clients may need to be helped to learn how to use the sessions productively. This is apt to be particularly true with clients who come from economically or educationally deprived backgrounds. When the client and the social worker do have a shared culture, which may be signaled by a sense of "ordinariness" (Bruner 1983), the client's need for inter-psychic space will be reduced.

Clinical Illustration

Tracking interpsychic space is actually not a new or strange endeavor for the clinical social worker. It is essentially the foundation for the interviewing skills that have been taught for years to new professionals from process recording. A brief example is nevertheless provided in order to show the manner in which these principles can be applied. Since frequent shifts in the interpsychic space are most common in clients with borderline patterns of the self, the principles are easiest to illustrate in an example involving a client with that pattern.

When approached in the waiting room, Margaret (see Chapter 7) was a little slow in removing her Walkman, but when she had done so she smiled, reached out for a handshake, and said "You must be Mrs. M."

The social worker agreed, smiling, and said "Will you come with me, Mrs. T?" Once in the worker's office, Margaret hesitated for a moment as if deciding where she wanted to sit. Attempting to welcome her, the social worker said, "Have a seat."

Margaret glanced questioningly at the chair closest to the social worker's and asked, "Here?"

"Anywhere you like," the worker replied. Margaret seated herself in the chair and looked expectantly at the worker, who asked, "Can you tell me what has brought you here?"

"Well, Dr. Smith suggested I come." Margaret stopped for a moment here as if to see if the social worker wanted to take over or already knew what Dr. Smith wanted. Since the social worker was simply waiting, Margaret shook her head, had a pained expression on her face, and averted her eyes from the social worker's face while continuing with,

"There's just so much, I don't know where to begin." Another brief moment passed, and Margaret almost pleadingly looked at the social worker, saying, "My brain feels like a sponge. I can't take anymore."

The worker asked, "Is there something you are afraid will happen?"

"Well, yes, you see I've been taking college classes for the last few months. I've always wanted to become a teacher. But I wake up in the morning with a headache—they're horrible headaches. There are so many problems, and I guess I'm scared I won't be able to keep up with the classes."

Therapy is a new situation for Margaret, and she is not sure about what will happen here. There is a question about how well her previous representations will match this context. As a result she is cautious, and her hesitation in taking off her Walkman allows her the opportunity to assume control of the initial interaction. Once in the office, Margaret is not sure how physically close she wants to be to the social worker (physical distance can be seen as a metaphor for interpsychic distance). The social worker's response tells Margaret that she can be in charge of how close she wants to be, a response that helps the boundaries of Margaret's transitional self open more. Margaret reacts as if she may now think this is not going to be a threatening place.

The social worker's question as to what brought her here, however, places a demand on Margaret to communicate the content of her meaning system. This is uncomfortable for her since her inner life at the moment is confused and threatened with becoming overwhelmed. Margaret chooses to begin with the fact that Dr. Smith sent her—a more impersonal subject than her own feelings and therefore one that is safer. No doubt Margaret hopes/fears that the social worker will respond to her comment about Dr. Smith and keep the interaction on the more factual and interpsychically distant level of her physical condition and Dr. Smith's reasons for the referral.

If the social worker had asked about the referral it would not have been a terrible therapeutic error especially since she does want to know about how Margaret's physical condition affects her capacity to create meaning. On the other hand, staying with the referral at this point in the interview might have given Margaret the message that the social worker was going to be comfortable only with a more distant interpsychic space. This social worker, therefore, chooses to wait, watching how the regulatory activities of Margaret's self will deal with this. What happens is that Margaret looks away from the social worker's face, thereby somewhat closing the boundaries of the transitional self, but then is able to refer to the organizational strain that the operational self is experiencing. Again the social worker does not intervene, until Margaret's resumption of eye contact and statement that she cannot take any more serves as a request for the social worker to help in the attempt to shore up the strain she is feeling.

This social worker's question regarding whether there is something that Margaret is afraid of is a particularly attuned response. It follows from the overt content of Margaret's presentation, and it also asks about the evaluative aspect of Margaret's meaning system. Since Margaret has already demonstrated her concerns about keeping the interpsychic space a safe one, the social worker already knows that the evaluative function of meaning is very active in Margaret's self. Thus, in asking about it, the social worker directs herself to the area of Margaret's concern. Margaret's answer tells the social worker much about just how severe and imminent the threat to the capacity to create meaning is that Margaret is experiencing. In this instance the social worker learned that Margaret has some ability to sustain functioning in an immediate sense but that she fears a longer-term effect—that of failing to function well in school. The social worker's question, however, can be expected to tell Margaret that the social worker has understood her dilemma in a very basic way. This is because the worker focused on the evaluative meaning of events for Margaret. Often, of course, much of this kind of communication occurs at an unconscious level, without either the client or the social worker having had time to formulate a picture of what is occurring.

In family and group therapy, of course, the worker tracks the interpsychic space between individuals in much the same manner. In those formats, however, the social worker is often observing interactions between clients and intervenes only when those immediately involved in the interactions need assistance.

III THE CONTENT OF IDENTITY

9 Narrative as the Organizer

Mrs. Jones enters a social worker's office and is asked to explain what it is that has brought her there. Mrs. Jones is then expected to tell the *story* behind whatever is troubling her, as well as what she believes might happen in the office that could help her. Social workers have been dealing in stories from the beginning of the profession. Until recently, however, clinical theory has taken the use of stories for granted, without sufficient examination of the nature and characteristics of the narrative form in which they are composed. In the past few years, however, narrative theory has been receiving considerable attention in other disciplines. The result is the availability of a body of thought that has much applicability to clinical practice.

In the past in social work there was a tendency to assume that the events of the story that Mrs. Jones tells existed in an intact form "out there." If anything seemed amiss with Mrs. Jones's story, it was assumed that there was something wrong with her skills in relating the story. The historian Hayden White (1980) has called attention to the fact that stories do not exist "out there" but must be constructed. A story contains a structure and an order of meaning that the events of the real world do not possess even if they are considered in temporal sequence. A pure chronology lists in order of sequence every event that may have occurred in a particular arena regardless of its importance or relevance to anything. In contrast, a story selects temporally ordered events according to their causal relevance for a particular end point.

Mrs. Jones will not tell the social worker everything that has occurred to her in her life. Indeed, she will not even talk about everything that has happened since she first identified a problem in her life. She will relate only that which she sees as having a significant relationship to the problem for which she seeks help, and she will organize this according to her own ideas about its cause. Since the personal problem that Mrs. Jones presents has to do with the relative safety of her existence as she experiences it, it may be said that the content of the story she tells is part of her identity. Furthermore, the particular end point that the events of the story will have been selected to demonstrate is her evaluation of her state at present.

If Mrs. Jones is experiencing herself as a competent and fortunate woman, and wants the social worker to view her that way, she may choose to tell of her recent promotion on her job and of having been valedictorian of her high school class. If she is experiencing herself as lonely and depressed, she may tell of her abusive mother and her problems in getting along with her husband. All of these and myriad other events may have occurred in Mrs. Jones' life, but the social worker will hear only that which bears on Mrs. Jones as she now sees herself. A story can therefore be seen to originate not at the beginning but, rather, at the end. It is from the perspective of the ending that the events to be included are selected. The evaluative end point of the stories that clients tell in treatment concerns the content of their identity as they are currently experiencing it.

Clinical social workers, however, have never simply accepted the stories of their clients as these are presented. Knowing that clients "forget" to talk about information that may have an important bearing on the problem as the social worker might view it, social workers routinely ask specific questions about the problem and/or about the client's life the answers to which must then be woven into the client's story. In this manner the social worker directly affects the client's narrative and the content of the client's identity. In the end the narratives about the client and the treatment that the social worker and the client will separately tell may not be identical, but both participants in the interaction will have played a part in constructing the content of both stories.

Even from this brief and simple overview it should be clear that an understanding of narrative is central to clinical social work theory.

Characteristics of Narrative

Narrative seems to be ubiquitous in human culture. Mancuso and Sarbin (1983) have noted that human beings think, perceive, imagine, and dream in a narrative structure. White (1980) has referred to narrative as a universal metacode on the basis of which transcultural messages about the nature of a shared reality can be transmitted. Certainly, the content of a story varies from individual to individual and from culture to culture, but the telling of stories is common to all cultures.

There is some controversy in the literature as to how much story structure varies from one culture to another. Different notions of time, for example, may lead to different narrative structures. In a discussion of Emily's tape recordings (see Chapter 5), Nelson (1989) made the following comments:

> As Whorf (1956) argued, based on evidence from Hopi, time is not treated in all linguistic systems as a system of linearly arranged units, but may be alternatively treated as a stream of recurrent events. It may seem overly speculative to suggest that Emily's early protonarratives could as well be organized within that system as within the "Standard Average European" (SAE) "time-line." I base this suggestion on the total lack of evidence that Emily distinguishes in these early passages whether events happened on one occasion or on many occasions, were or were not distinct from one another, might or might not happen again. Rather, her monologues up to the middle of her twenty-fourth month suggest that her notion of events in time is quite undifferentiated. (p. 300)

Ong (1982) has argued that the temporal ordering of narrative form is not inherent in the human brain but that human beings become trained for this in literate societies. This possibility should be kept in mind. However, the vast majority of social work clients clearly do come from and participate in cultures utilizing a linear temporal model for narrative organization.

Stories, as Mandler (1984) pointed out, are organized according to temporal and/or causal relationships. This is different from the traditionally understood organization of thought through categories and may be more basic to the organization of thought than categories. In order to form a story structure the individual must abstract part of the whole of events in accord with what is significant to the point being made. In contrast, the type of abstraction

used in the formation of categories is based on principles of similarity. Mandler and Nelson both basically argue that the part/
whole relationship is easier for children to grasp than the principle
of similarity and is mastered first developmentally.

The literature contains a number of different ways of conceptualizing the elements in a story. In his classic *Grammar of
Motives*, Kenneth Burke (1945) recognized that story structure
minimally contains an agent, an action, a goal, a setting, and an
instrument. More recently, Labov (1972) has described a fully
formed narrative as including the following: (1) an abstract or brief
summary of the whole story; (2) an orientation that sets time, place,
characters, and so forth; (3) an action that complicates something
described in the orientation; (4) an evaluation; (5) a result or resolution; and (6) a coda or signal that the narrative is finished and
that brings the speaker back to the present time.

Stories may have many episodes, some of which may be im-
bedded or interleaved with one another, so that there may be
many attempts at reaching one goal or a number of subgoals. The
outcome may also have many facets that are interrelated. Stories
spell out cause-and-effect relationships; goals and goal-seeking
behavior; connections between events, people, and places; conflict
resolution; and human intentions and expectations. Polanyi (1979)
perhaps put all of this most succinctly by indicating that narratives
have three types of information: (1) event structure, which serves
to keep time; (2) descriptive structure, which contains all of the
environmental and character-centered information; and (3) evaluative structure, which contains what the narrator considers to be
the crucial information in the story.

Good story making is a heuristic process that requires skill,
judgment, and experience. It consists of using culturally acceptable
concepts to create a fit between a situation and the story schema.
When it is successful, the result is a coherent and plausible account
of how and why something happened. A successful story about
everyday life is not a fiction in that it gives organization to experienced or observed occurrences. On the other hand, the causal
implications involved in a story definitely do not have the status of
causality as this concept is understood in science. Whereas in
science that which is considered a cause is expected to be the
necessary and sufficient condition to produce a given result,
it is inherent in the nature of stories that any one story is only
one version of many possible ways of accounting for the same
events.

It is possible through narrative construction to create a tapestry of meaning with richly woven interconnections of various sorts. Such construction relies, of course, on the possibility of a series of episodes involving subordinate plots, goals, scenes, and characters, all of which can be complexly interrelated and descriptively developed. In this manner stories can convey a much more extensive body of information than can any purely categorical hierarchy and can make explicit the connections between the various dissimilar elements in a way that the construction of categorical information can not. Mink (1978) has pointed out that the function of narrative form is "to body forth an ensemble of interrelationships of many different kinds as a single whole" (p. 144).

A well-constructed story, then, uses a vast array of types of information to create a coherent whole in which the events chosen for the story provide a logical explanation for the occurrence of the end point of the story (Mancuso & Sarbin, 1983). Current psychological theory emphasizes the human need to experience the self as cohesive (Kohut, 1971); from this perspective it becomes clear that experiencing the self as a well-functioning unit is highly dependent upon the ability of the individual to construct an integrated and coherent narrative about the self, which is here being called identity. Bruner (1987) explains the relationship between autobiographical narative and identity:

> The heart of my argument is this: eventually the culturally shaped cognitive and linguistic processes that guide the self-telling of life narratives achieve the power to structure perceptual experience, to organize memory, to segment and purpose-build the very "events" of a life. In the end, we *become* the autobiographical narratives by which we "tell about" our lives. (p. 15)

Schafer (1980) has pointed out that not only do human beings create themselves through the narration of their lives but they create the others with whom they interact through narration as well. Therefore, in treatment the clinician does not know how an uninvolved external observer would describe the interaction between a client and one of the significant others that client describes. What the clinician knows instead is the self and other that the client has created through the narrative. The most reliable clue that the clinician has regarding how the client relates to his or her significant others is the manner in which the client relates to the therapist, rather than the content of the stories the client tells of these others. On the other hand, the content of the stories provides valuable information about how clients experience others as well as themselves in interactions with others. An understanding of both of these elements is, of course, essential for good treatment.

Identity and Clients' Stories

The context in which a story is told invariably affects the nature and meaning of the story. In a clinical setting it can be assumed that, whatever the overt content of the story, the end point of the story invariably contains a message to the clinician about the manner in which the client is currently experiencing himself or herself. Stories told in treatment, therefore, can all be considered to be representative of the client's attempts at identity construction. Knowing from the outset that there are many ways to tell a story about similar content, the clinician's concern is not with whether or not the story is "true" in a literal scientific sense but, rather, with influencing the content of the story so that it will be more useful to the client's functioning.

Narrative has the capacity to organize interrelationships of many different kinds into a coherent whole, and it is through the utilization of narrative form that the multiple senses of a complex identity are integrated. It is assuredly no accident that Erikson's (1958, 1969) psychological studies read like very persuasive biographical stories. Narrative form, serves as the organizing activity that Hartmann (1957) ascribed to the synthetic function of the ego. Skills in the construction of stories about oneself are therefore central to the experience of an integrated and coherent identity.

The discussion by Agar and Hobbs (1982) of coherence in narrative is useful in considering the degree of integration in any particular client's story telling. They identify three different levels of coherence in narratives. The first is *local coherence*, where each successive utterance is tied to prior ones by syntactic, temporal, or causal relations. The second is *global coherence*, where statements exemplify or move forward the overall intent or point of the story. The third is *themal coherence*, where the statements serve as expressions of generalized cultural issues.

Narrated identity content is not static but must be constantly rewritten and reorganized in order to reflect the end point of the present (Gergen & Gergen, 1987). For this reason, the client's story can always be considered to represent the manner in which the client is experiencing himself or herself in the present, including the relative degree of comfort or safety and the level of currently experienced self-esteem. Since the content of the client's stories can be expected to change from one session to another, indeed from one segment of the same session to another, paying attention to the content of the client's stories is one way to follow shifts in the client's experience of self. Small shifts in content or emphasis may often reflect slight shifts in the experience of the self of which the client may be quite unaware. Shifts in the content of the stories is, in fact, one important manner of tracking the client's progress in treatment.

The purpose of treatment is to help the client practice the creation of meaning. A negative evaluation either of the safety of the self or of self-esteem is likely to reduce the level of energy devoted to the creation of meaning. For this reason, the clinician needs to be sure that the content of the sessions, as expressed by either participant, is not demeaning to or too harshly critical of the client. This does not, of course, mean that negative behavior and unfavorable aspects of the client's experience or situation should be ignored or treated in a Pollyanna-like fashion. In particular, it is important to accept the client's evaluation of himself or herself, since creating doubts in the client's mind about the ability to make such evaluations will also be counterproductive. Thus, harsh self-judgments can be accepted as being perhaps sad but as not telling the whole story or as being potentially surmountable in the future.

Although the social worker will inevitably influence the content of the client's identity, it is important to remember that identity construction is an active process that can usefully be carried out only by the individual involved. In a discussion of the importance of fairy stories to children, Bettelheim (1976) made the following comment:

> Adult interpretation, as correct as they may be, rob the child of the opportunity to feel that he, on his own through repeated hearing and ruminating about the story, has coped successfully with a difficult situation. We grow, we find meaning in life, and security in ourselves by having understood and solved personal problems on our own, not by having them explained to us by others. (p. 19)

The same principle applies to all therapy in that it is the client who must construct his or her own identity. The clinician contributes to the content but does so by paying attention to contradictions, gaps, and evasions in the content of the story; unexplored possibilities or implications of the story; and other ways of framing or constructing the story (Schafer, 1983).

The basic reason that the content of identity is important is not because of any presumed accuracy in regard to causative factors from the past but, rather, because it constitutes the perspective from which the client will select behavior in the future (Mancuso & Sarbin, 1983). The content of the client's stories will therefore always reflect the individual's particular pattern of meaning making, including that person's characteristic use of selective perception and difficulty in organizing or experiencing the material. For this reason the clinician will always utilize a diagnosis of the individual's pattern of the self to guide both the timing and the content of interventions. All interventive content will therefore be selected on the basis of its cumulative ability to enhance the capacity to create meaning.

Intervention strategy and content must be tailored to an understanding of the specific functioning of the client as an individual. In arriving at an understanding of the individual, however, the clinician will be greatly aided by an understanding of the types of content-related problems often encountered in people with common deficits in the capacity to create meaning as these affect narratives.

Psychotic Functioning

In acute psychotic states the capacity to create meaning has collapsed. As Eissler (1952) long ago noted in work with individuals in such states, the clinician needs to convey confidence in the possibility of meaningfulness. For that reason, the specific interpretive cast of the meaning that the clinician may use need not be the central concern. Instead, interacting in a manner that will assist the client in achieving a comfortable degree of interpsychic space and in a manner that will demonstrate that meaning of some sort is possible is indicated.

Narrative construction is dependent upon a stable system of preexisting event representations. For the psychotic person, retaining event representations in an intact and usable form is difficult. That which seems meaningful at one moment may threaten to disappear or be shown to be totally false at another. The result is an extraordinarily terrifying state in which the person is likely to feel as if he or she is drowning in a sea of indistinguishable stimuli. In other words, the person is threatened with a state of perpetual pathologic merger.

The "I" of identity is a narrative construction; so also is the "you" of the object. At the same time, it is the sense of identity that provides the basic organizing point from which a narrative can be organized; a story requires a narrator and a point of view. With the collapse of the capacity to create meaning, the acutely psychotic person is caught in the double bind of being unable to create an identity because of an inability to narrate and with an inability to narrate because of a lack of a stable sense of an "I" who could tell the story. Under these circumstances it hardly seems surprising that in psychosis the fundamental fear is that of annihilation.

It is likely that in infancy the original "I" of identity exists only as a "you" in the mind of the caretaker (Sullivan, 1953). The very first identity narratives are told not by the infant but by the caretaker who verbalizes for the infant simple tales about what the baby has done within the formats of early interaction. Thus, it may be that the first category that the child abstracts is that of persons, with "I" and "You" as appropriate slot fillers. Thus, as the infant gradually achieves some sense of stable event representations, the first sense of a personal existence and identity is also constructed. As Litowitz and Litowitz (1983) have indicated, however, this first sense of identity is probably not that of a self as an object or even as a subject but, rather, as a participant in an interpersonal dialogue.

From this perspective, it follows that the first goal of a clinician in working with an acutely psychotic individual should be to help that person reconstitute a stable sense of identity as a participant in an interpersonal dialogue. On the surface, this may sound as if it could easily be accomplished; this is, of course, not so. The operational self of the psychotic person is easily overwhelmed, and the transitional self may be rigidly closed in order to protect from overstimulation. Thus, helping the individual with psychotic functioning to participate in a true dialogue is a major undertaking. In attempting to do so, however, keeping a content focus on the fact that there are two separate individuals with notably different characteristics involved in the interactions is apt to be helpful in averting pathological mergers.

The grandiosity of persons with psychotic functioning generally involves the sense that everything in the world has a personal meaning or message for them. This kind of thinking is often deprecated in that it seems extremely self-centered and therefore socially nonfunctional. On the other hand, all elements in a story do have a personal significance for the narrator; otherwise, the narrator would not have chosen to include them. It is easier to treat the person with psychotic functioning if it is understood that the grandiosity is, in fact, an attempt at constituting a fundamental sense of existence so that a meaningful identity can be constructed. While this grandiosity may have negative results in interactions within a current social milieu, the individual needs to be encouraged to continue the underlying attempt at constructing personal meaning, but in ways that can be tolerated by potential partners in a dialogue.

It should be readily apparent that without stable event representations, causal thinking that is logical is impossible. The person with psychotic functioning can, therefore, have little sense of cause-and-effect relationships. Much of what has been considered magical thinking can be understood as a failure in the ability to understand the existence of a chain of temporally ordered events, some of which may not be immediately observable, that leads to the particular result in question. Word magic—that is, thinking that saying or thinking a word can make the associated event happen—is a similar phenomenon. There is something of an observable basis to word magic in that clearly verbal communication to another person ("pass the salt," for example) does, in a sense, make it happen. Extending the power of language beyond the realm of interpersonal requests is simply another manifestation of faulty cause-and-effect relationships.

Delusions can be understood to be narrative constructions that often involve an elaboration of faulty causal notions. Frequently, such constructions require enormous effort to build, and they serve the purpose of fending off total meaninglessness. Therefore, the entire construction must be rigidly maintained. It is as if the delusional person believes that if anything at all is discovered to be wrong with any aspect of the formulation, it all must be abandoned. The person is not able to alter smaller aspects of a story in order to adjust it to experience changes in the environment. Major challenges to the content of meaning constructions will therefore be resisted and will, in fact, be unhelpful to the client. Instead, the clinician must suggest the possibility of small additions to the content, usually in the form of observations by the clinician that are offered without any pressure for the client to adopt or endorse them.

Character-Disordered Functioning

Persons who function with character-disordered patterns of meaning making normally have some stable event representations, but these are not sufficiently well established to allow for their use in more advanced cognitive processing. Lexical/semantic language is, therefore, used by individuals with character-disordered functioning largely for its ability to help control the environment, particularly the interpersonal environment. While there may be considerable skill in using language (to influence the therapist, for example), there will be little ability to use it in relation to a world of personally experienced meaning, to capture feelings, or even to contemplate an evaluation of abstracted qualities of the external world.

Because of these limitations, the stories told in therapy by character-disordered individuals are often temporally ordered scripts rather than true narratives. Early attempts at story telling by children also take the form of temporally ordered scripts. Nelson (1986) described the difference between children's scripts and narratives in the following manner:

> In contrast, children's scripts are general timeless accounts told from the point of view of the narrator without necessarily specifying mental or emotional states, actions or motivations; involving no problem to be solved but only a routine to be followed. Whereas the same event structure may form the basis for both a script and a story, the narration of one or the other will be very different. Scripts will be produced in the timeless present tense, in the order in which actions occur, and without details of time, place, or characters. Beginnings and endings will be very simple (e.g. "First you ...," "That's all"). Stories are told in the past tense, provide specific characters, present a problem and its resolution, and often have conventional beginnings and endings. (p. 163)

The scripts of character-disordered individuals differ from those of children in that they are usually told in the past tense, provide details about time and place, and may include a description of the characters from an external point of view, that is, with only a superficial account of a character's motivation or intention. Motivation or intention will usually be understood only in terms of attempts to control the environment in order to obtain conditions necessary for continued functioning. Without an understanding of the internal world of other human beings, the person with character-disordered functioning will be able to abstract routines to be followed on the basis of event representations but will not be able to modify these in accord with affective states. Thus, social control is conceived of as being achieved through an external reward–punishment system and through the existence of externally formulated rules rather than through internalized values or goals.

The major difference between the scripts produced by character-disordered persons in treatment and true narratives, however, is often seen in the difficulty character-disordered persons have in selecting a well-established evaluative end point from which to begin the story and in choosing the significant events. In treatment, therefore, character-disordered persons often spend time relating in temporal order the events that have occurred to them since the last contact. Such recitals frequently seem boring to the clinician because the point of the story is not evident. In fact, of course, what the client is attempting to do, rather than begin with an evaluation of the self, is to master the ability to abstract an evaluation of the self based on the events that have occurred. In a sense, these clients live in a world of action without a sense of identity, without a sense of being able to truly exert control over the course of events, without either a future or a past.

Specifically, because of the lack of evaluative conclusions—or, in some cases, because of the existence of superficial, hastily constructed, but rigidly adhered-to conclusions—in the content of material produced by character-disordered individuals, therapeutic work with them can be extremely tedious for the clinician. There is a tendency to want simply to impose conclusions; the clinician's doing so will not infrequently be invited by the client, since having conclusions externally imposed relieves the client of the burden of the effort at construction. At times the therapist may in fact need to provide some social referencing along with acting as a soothing self-regulator. However, such social referencing leaves the client with the possibility of rejecting the evaluation should that seem pragmatically expedient at some point. In the long run the client will need to learn to formulate his or her own evaluations.

For the individual with character-disordered functioning, learning to include an evaluative structure within the personal narrative is difficult because there is so little ability to tolerate affect, particularly anxiety or negatively toned affect. Attempts on the part of the clinician to encourage the client to evaluate in more depth may be met with derisive refusals to believe there may be more than surface meaning in something or may result in dangerous acting-out behavior if the affective meaning is sensed but experienced as threatening. Successful long-term therapy with such individuals invariably seems to involve a period of experienced depression, which can be uncomfortable for both the client and the clinician but in which affect tolerance is greatly increased. In work with individuals with character disorders, therefore, the therapist's focus needs to be on the evaluative meaning of events for the self of the client, but the pace of the therapy must be in accordance with the degree of achieved affect tolerance and may have to move at a very slow pace.

Borderline Functioning

Ordinarily, persons with borderline functioning have stable event representations and have no difficulty with the temporal structure of story construction. The descriptive structure of their stories may vary considerably. For some individuals the excessive attention paid to affective communication and the affective coloration of the environment may lead to some denial in relation to concrete and inanimate aspects of the world. Causal formulations can therefore seem overly personalized and peculiar.

The main problem with narrative construction for individuals with borderline functioning, however, lies in a difficulty in being able to maintain a consistent end point for the story. Thus, the guide by which the story elements are selected is apt to shift in the middle of the telling. Persons with borderline functioning are so hypersensitive to affective communication and the evaluative meaning of the interpersonal context in which the story is told that a consistent story line is hard to maintain. The frequent shifting results in an identity that is experienced as chaotic. Content interpretations on the part of the therapist often serve the function of helping the client retain a focus to the narrative, even when this was not the conscious intent of the clinician. Consistency and predictability in the therapeutic environment and cutting down on the need for hypervigilance about the safety of the self and on the shifts in the sense of identity that serves as the story's end point are greatly facilitating for people with borderline pathology. Having a relatively stable and nonthreatening environment within which to sort through the various aspects of the experienced inner chaos enables the person to begin to build some inner organization.

In the initial phases of treatment, individuals with borderline pathology will often seem very involved in the therapeutic relationship. However, once they truly feel secure within that relationship they may put much more interpsychic space between themselves and the clinician. Not infrequently, this involves canceled or failed appointments or a display of some hostile behavior toward the therapist. It is critical for the therapist to understand that this need for more interpsychic space while the client is working on a reorganization of existing inner life is not an indication that the treatment is not going well but, rather, is a necessary part of it, since it allows for concentrated attention on the inner experience. Too often, treatment with such individuals has been prematurely terminated out of the therapist's failure to appreciate the client's need to construct his or her own narrative while in a therapeutic relationship.

Persons with borderline patterns of meaning making generally are very much aware of their inner life. Furthermore, their language usually has a direct relationship to the inner states they wish to represent. For this reason, the effort of putting experience into words, which characterizes most of traditional treatment practice, is constructive for them in that it helps organize inner life and therefore contain it.

Language usage by borderline individuals may often seem creative or even flowery specifically because the attempt is to find words that can capture an inner life that is experienced although confused. For this reason word meaning may be quite individualized rather than based on shared cultural/lexical meaning. Clinicians who work regularly with this population usually learn quickly to check out word meaning in order to be sure that there is true client–social worker understanding. In the process of such negotiation over meaning, of course, the client learns to negotiate with significant others outside the therapy as well. This is an extremely important process, since part of the sense of being alone— of which individuals with borderline problems frequently complain—derives from an inability to communicate well with, and thereby to obtain social validation from, a broader human community because of a lack of skill in using the lexical/semantic structure.

Narcissistic Functioning

Individuals with borderline patterns of meaning making may have difficulty in tolerating the experienced chaos that is involved in the autobiographical narratives they are able to create. In contrast, individuals with narcissistic patterns have an inordinate difficulty in being able to create a personally meaningful narrative. Not infrequently, narcissistic individuals are avid consumers of literature and other narratives about human beings. This interest seems largely motivated by an underlying hope for material that will have personal affective relevance for them. However, because the words in the stories seem to register almost totally at a lexical/semantic level with little connection to the conceptual level of personal experience, the forays into personal stories have little real yield for an understanding of themselves or the significant others with whom they interact.

In therapy some people with narcissistic disorders can relate stories superficially rather well. The structure of such stories will certainly not be as disorganized as those told by individuals with borderline pathology and may even be quite well constructed. Missing elements are likely, of course, to involve an understanding of intentionality or the subtle influences of affective communication on human interactions. Additionally, the stories may be used primarily for their potential to impress the therapist with personal access to material wealth or powerful people. The problem, of course, with these stories is that they do not serve identity functions, since they are glib and not truly experienced as personally relevant.

Work with narcissistic individuals, therefore, requires that the therapist not be too invested in the pure content of the narrative but, rather, that he or she pay attention to the accompanying nonverbal affective communication and focus on this whenever possible. In the long run, the goal must be to establish a connection between words and affective sensations. This is, of course, very demanding for the clinician.

On the other hand, the special value that the person with narcissistic problems places on words can also be used therapeutically. If the client has nonverbal interactive experiences with the therapist that have strongly positive affective meaning and these can be captured within a referential language shared by the client and the therapist, the words involved will often be used by the client almost like a mantra. The client will use the words to call up soothing inner sensations reminiscent of the experience in therapy. This can then serve as a beginning connection between words and an experienced inner life.

10 The Uses of History

One of the fundamental ideas in Freud's theory of psychoanalysis was that present pathology could be understood as a regression to a previous stage of psychosexual development. This principle, taken in concert with the idea that memory is accurate, led to an assumption that it was possible for the clinician to know the causes of problems in current functioning from the client's account of his or her history. In recent years, of course, the accuracy of the client's history has been called into serious question (Schafer, 1983; Spence, 1982). A scientific understanding of causal relationships among possible etiological agents must be established in studies that are designed specifically for this purpose rather than in single clinical examples.

A client may provide a history in which some events fit well with research findings. For example, a woman who has dissociative experiences may report memories of sexual abuse by a close relative. In examples of this sort, the social worker is likely to believe that the incestuous relationship probably contributed to the causation of the dissociative experiences. While this is not an outlandish assumption, it does not and cannot have the status of true scientific causality. The social worker will have to gear the treatment toward relief of the dissociative symptoms of the present, knowing that their precise causality may never be known.

Mitchell (1988) has argued that not only has psychoanalytic theory's reliance on metaphorical reference to infancy lulled therapists into a false confidence that they understood the causation of the problems they encountered but that psychoanalysis has also led to an infantilizing of clients. He believes that therapy is best understood as a process involving the further development of the person in the present, rather than as either a recapitulation of or a regression to earlier life stages.

If the best attempts of the client and the therapist together do not result in an accurate and scientific picture of the client's past and of the causation of the client's problems, why bother to take a history at all? If therapy is not understood as a recapitulation of earlier life stages, as a process in which problems from earlier experiences can be repaired, why spend so much time in therapy trying to understand what might have happened in the past?

A number of years ago Novey (1968) argued that the reason for paying attention to the past in therapy is that the present has been shaped by what has happened in the past. While this argument has a certain ring of common sense to it, the specific manner in which a clinician can understand and use history needs more explication.

Identity and the Future

Understanding that the histories clients provide in therapy are really narrative accounts of who they now are and how they became that way—that is, recognizing that these stories actually constitute the content of their current identities—makes an important difference in the way the histories are understood theoretically. While not scientifically accurate views of causality or of the past, these stories do provide the clinician with an understanding of the client's view of his or her environment and of his or her relationship to it, as well as of the causal and interpersonal interactions within it. A client's history also provides a picture of the level of security, effectance, and self-esteem that accompanies the client's evaluation of his or her current situation.

If, in fact, the client's history constitutes that person's identity, then it becomes clear why the therapist needs to pay careful attention to it. Without the identity/history the clinician does not know who the client is and cannot form a relationship with that person. One cannot form a human relationship on the basis of a diagnosis, either the type in the American Psychiatric Association's diagnostic and statistical manual or the diagnostic patterns described in Chapter 7. A relationship is, after all, based on the meaning that is created between two people and cannot occur in the absense of a consideration of the meaning systems of the individuals involved. The therapist who does not listen carefully to the client's history will not know the client as that person experiences himself or herself.

A person's narrated identity is not so much an accurate account of what it is that has happened in the past as it is a blueprint on the basis of which the individual will carry out social relationships. It is the foundation for the person's understanding of how he or she wishes to act in the social roles available within the social system and of what goals he or she wishes to pursue within that arena. The client's autobiographical narrative contains implications not just for the past and the present but for the future as well.

> The impact of reconstructions and hence of the way one's past is seen cannot be overestimated as a force in determining the course of future events. The very concept of history as a predictive instrument suggests that today's view of history will influence tomorrow's course of events. (Novey, 1986, p. 149)

Gergen and Gergen (1983, 1987) have pointed out that narratives can be (1) progressive, in that the protagonist is conceived of as continuing to develop or achieve; (2) regressive, in that the protagonist or the situation is deteriorating; or (3) stable, in that the protagonist and his or her situation are not undergoing change. Clients generally seek the services of a clinical social worker because they are unhappy in some sense. This discontent is not just with isolated events in their lives, since these could be tolerated if they were experienced as temporary or inconsequential. Instead, clients believe that their lives are not moving toward some goal that they either have consciously formulated or take for granted. In other words, they want what they feel they do not have: an identity that involves at least a stable narrative, or, more hopefully, a progressive one.

Successful therapy essentially involves the creation, through the collaboration of the client and the therapist, of an identity that involves a life narrative in which the client is seen as progressing toward his or her chosen goal. Having an identity that involves a progressive narrative does not, of course, guarantee that the person will eventually achieve the implied goal. Many environmental circumstances and future events beyond the control of either the client or the therapist may intervene to facilitate or impede its achievement. At times, the goal may need to be adjusted. It may be too ambitious when viewed in the light of the resources available to the client. Conversely, it may be that in the light of the client's actual talents and opportunities the goal is insufficiently imaginative. In either case, the therapeutic activity involves the selection and ordering of events such that the resulting narrative has either a stable or a progressive tone. A brief clinical example will help make this clearer.

Mrs. P, an attractive 32-year-old widow with two young children, entered therapy at the urging of a neighbor and close friend who was concerned over Mrs. P's depression and lack of activity. Mrs. P's husband had been killed suddenly in an automobile accident one year previously. Insurance benefits had left Mrs. P without serious financial concerns, enabling her to remain at home taking care of the preschool children. However, she had withdrawn from most activities outside of the home, so that she was quite isolated socially. Mrs. P had been feeling that her life was basically over and that nothing she could now do would bring her happiness.

Mrs. P presented herself initially as uncertain if therapy was a good idea, since perhaps paying attention to her state of mind was a waste of time and money. When this was challenged, Mrs. P was able to say that she thought getting over her husband's death had been made harder by the fact that they had had an argument that was left unresolved on the morning he had been killed. She knew this probably had nothing to do with the cause of the accident, since it had not been her husband's fault, but it left her with an intense regret that their relationship had ended in that way.

Mrs. P described the marriage as primarily satisfying to her, acknowledging that her husband had been a kind and patient man who often had to put up with her moodiness. She regretted that she had been denied a chance to tell him how much she had loved him before he died. At the same time, she knew that he would want her to get on with her life, but somehow she did not feel as if she could do so. She worried that her depression might be hard on the children, who knew that she was not happy. Soon both children would be in school most of the day; Mrs. P thought she probably should look for some work to do during that time, but she had no enthusiasm for doing so.

Mrs. P's history included being the oldest child of parents who also had a reasonably good relationship. Her childhood had been fairly pleasant until her brother, 5 years her junior, was diagnosed as having congenital heart problems when she was 8 years old. At that time her parents began focusing much energy and attention on her brother. His condition had steadily worsened, however, and when Mrs. P was 12 he died. Both parents had been extremely depressed over this death, and Mrs. P believed that neither had ever fully recovered from the loss.

Mrs. P had been a good student in grammar school but in high school was only mediocre and was more involved in her social life. She had been seen as an attractive girl and had many dates. Against her parents' wishes she had married immediately after high school and moved away from home with her husband. She described this first marriage as a disaster; her husband, who had seemed charming and fun-loving in high school, could not keep a job and became insanely jealous of and abusive to her. After 2 years she obtained a divorce but remained in the area to which she and her husband had moved, more because she felt ashamed to return to her hometown than because she felt any particular liking for the new location. Mrs. P described the 4 years after the divorce and before she became involved with Mr. P as miserable. She had worked as a receptionist but hated the job because she was bored. She felt isolated and uninvolved socially. Following her second marriage Mrs. P had worked until early in her first pregnancy, when she had been happy to quit. She thought of the years at home with the children before her husband's death as the happiest time of her life.

Since Mrs. P seemed to be immobilized by the death of her husband, her social worker's focus in the early phase of treatment was on her experience with her brother's death as well as her husband's. Mrs. P described her brother as a good kid who had been patient with all the medical procedures and who deserved the family's attention during his illness. She could not recall having resented the attention he received before his death, but when this possibility was suggested to her by the social worker, she could imagine that she might have. Mrs. P recalled having worked very hard to be good during her brother's illness and being very angry at her parents after his death. She and her therapist agreed that probably she had hoped for attention and appreciation for her efforts from her parents following her brother's death. However, this attention had not been forthcoming, since her parents remained in a state of distress over the death.

In the course of the client–therapist discussions, Mrs. P came to feel that she had been in part rebelling against her parents in her lack of interest in school as an adolescent. She had received much attention from boyfriends at that time, but she ended up with a somewhat wild group of youngsters of whom her parents had not approved. She thought this accounted for the bad choice she had made in her first marriage.

Mrs. P agreed with her social worker that she was now dealing with two deaths—that of her brother and her husband. In fact, Mrs. P noted, she had not thought of it before but in some ways her husband, a quiet and gentle man, had been similar to her brother. She felt both had died before she could tell them of her love for them. The therapist noted that Mrs. P now acted as if she did not deserve the attention she had so much wanted but did not get after her brother died. Was she perhaps fearful that if she dealt with her sadness through getting attention socially, she would only make things worse by getting into another disastrous relationship? Mrs. P thought this made some sense.

As Mrs. P thought back to her adolescence, she began to regret the fact that she had wasted her time in school. As a child she had wanted to go to college and become a teacher, a goal her parents had endorsed. In time, Mrs. P decided to arrange for increased day care for her youngest child so that she could begin college classes, with the goal of becoming a teacher. Mrs. P found her classes stimulating and terminated her treatment shortly after beginning this new phase of her life. She hoped she might someday meet another man she would want to marry but thought life could be satisfying if she did not.

Mrs. P entered treatment at a time when the sudden death of her husband had made impossible the future she had envisioned for herself. Her life narrative now had become a negative one, with an expectation that she would continue to be unhappy. It was, however, impossible for her to function well in the present with this persepctive. Since Mrs. P did not have a specific goal toward which to work in her life narrative, it became necessary for the therapy to work toward the selection of one. Such a goal must, of course, not be imposed by the clinicican but must emerge from the client's meaning system.

Mrs. P's life narrative could not be altered without first having some idea of how she arrived at the particular evaluation she had reached, namely, that life would continue to be unhappy. Mrs. P understood that her first experience with unhappiness involved the illness and death of her brother. The social worker then selected this event to focus on as the "narrative point of origin" (Stern, 1985). In other words, this event was granted the status of causal agency within the story to be constructed. Although the problems around her brother's death probably did have some causal status in relation to Mrs. P's personality, a truly scientific account of Mrs. P's development would have to consider many more factors, including biology, her environment long before her brother's diagnosis, and specific interactions with this environment.

While the fact that Mrs. P's brother's death had a profound impact on her is not untrue, the story that was constructed around this is only one way of understanding Mrs. P's life. This point of origin for the story leads to the explanation of why life is miserable for Mrs. P. In the process, however, of noticing how the story unfolded from that point in her life, Mrs. P was helped to see that her story might have been different if perhaps that event had not occurred or if other events had progressed differently after that time. In other words, she recognized that her life story could be organized with a different emphasis, with a different narrative point of origin. Mrs. P recalled that she had been a good student who wanted to be a teacher. She understood that this fact could be used as a new narrative point of origin in a different story. In the new story the goal could be to become a teacher and the death of the brother and the subsequent marriages could be subplots that explain why reaching the goal was such a long and arduous journey. In this new story there is a progressive narrative, one that can sustain a sense of accomplishment and self-esteem for Mrs. P.

The treatment ended before Mrs. P achieved her goal, and the social worker did not know if she would actually become a teacher or not. But a sense of purpose and meaningfulness had been restored to Mrs. P. If Mrs. P encounters difficulties en route to becoming a teacher, perhaps she will need to readjust her life story. If at that time she has more difficulty in doing this, she will perhaps need to seek treatment once again. In the future, however, Mrs. P may be able to make adjustments in her life story without the help of additional therapy. This is particularly likely since this woman's basic underlying capacity to create meaning was fairly well developed. Thus, the problems needing to be addressed were more in the realm of identity content than in the functioning of the self. In most cases, of course, the treatment must deal simultaneously with both self and identity.

Although there is no guarantee, the likelihood of Mrs. P's becoming a teacher greatly increased simply because this became the goal toward which she worked. There is an underlying principle here: if you want to achieve something in the future, you first have to create a past that will be consonant with that achievement as the outcome of the story. This is precisely what therapy does. It helps the client view his or her past from a point of view that makes the desired future more possible.

There are some instances, however, when the issue is not the creation of a new goal for the future but, rather, the creation of a life narrative in which the current outcome can be considered to be the result of a progressive or satisfactory narrative. This is the case in circumstances in which it does indeed appear unlikely that the client's current situation will change. This occurs, for example, in work with the elderly or the dying. Although the inevitability of death is unavoidable, the client can be helped, through a life review process, to shift both the selection of events that led to the current state and the evaluation of those events so that the story can end with the feeling that life was meaningful or satisfying.

Some clients have experienced lives that were full of failure or injustice, about which they may, understandably, have considerable anger. Therapy will not, of course, change the events of their lives, at least not from a purely objective point of view. Yet, since histories are constructed in the present and have the present as their end points, the context of the present will influence the point of view taken about the events of the past. This is where empathy or affect attunement and the contemplative but accepting environment of the client–therapist relationship become so important.

The therapist could not change the fact that Mrs. P's brother and husband were dead and that she had not told either one she loved him before he died. However, in the context of the treatment relationship Mrs. P could understand her failure to tell her loved ones of her feelings as an unfortunate circumstance rather than as evidence of her fundamental unworthiness. The past is unaltered, but the manner in which it is experienced has changed. The meaning of the past and its effect on the present have been modified. When viewed from the perspective that affect attunement can actually change the effects that the past has on the client, the almost awesome power of the relationship in therapy becomes apparent.

This clinical example clearly indicates that the therapist is not simply a passive recipient of the client's history. Although a clinician needs to listen carefully to the client's account of the history, he or she does not simply record it in a verbatim fashion. Instead, the clinician actively participates in the telling by asking questions that lead to clarifications about the relationships between events and to the inclusion of events that the client might otherwise have omitted. Clinical training has traditionally included the therapist's learning to collect, organize, and usually to write out an account of the client's history during an initial evaluative period. Yet not only is this history not a scientific account of the causes of the client's problems, it is not even a true representation of the client's identity, since it is the worker who organizes it. The end point of the story is the social worker's evaluation of the client, not the client's self-evaluation. What purpose, then, does a history of the client as constructed by the clinician serve?

In his classic paper on the therapeutic action of psychoanalysis, Loewald (1960) indicated that the therapist must relate to the client not as that person is at present but as that person can become in the future. Although the practice of constructing a history for the client has not generally been labeled as such in the past, it seems reasonable to think that the function that the therapist's history has always served has been that of a guideline for how the client can achieve a sense of self that is more organized, more highly articulated and integrated, and more conducive to a functional sense of self-esteem. In other words, the therapist constructs a more complex identity for the client than the client yet experiences in himself or herself.

The content of the client's identity is the focus of negotiation between the client and the therapist throughout treatment. The client's stories initially provide the therapist with a sense of how the unique and individual client under consideration actually experiences himself or herself, so that a relationship with that person can be formed. Within that relationship the therapist then formulates a picture of who the client may become in the future; by relating to the client as more than that person currently experiences himself or herself to be, the client does, in fact, gradually become more than he or she initially was.

It should be noted here that the material that is used to create a new identity for the client by no means comes exclusively from the client's initial historical account. The feedback that the client provides of interactions that occur in the current life situation provides additional information. This material has often been thought of as dealing with the client's present. However, since whatever the client reports to the therapist has already occurred (even if it only occurred a moment ago), current material is dealt with in therapy in precisely the same manner as the more distant past. Kierkegaard has been credited with recognizing that we live forward, but we understand backwards.

Narrative and the Cultural Context

Polanyi (1979) has demonstrated that only stories that contain culturally validated content can be persuasive to others. This makes sense in the light of Nelson's tripartite theory of meaning indicating that event representations, the most basic level of meaning upon which narratives are constructed, are acquired through participation in social activities and are therefore culturally specific. Categorical knowledge, which deals with the area of personal experience, is abstracted from event representations. Human identity in a personal sense, therefore, cannot be constructed in the absense of knowledge of the culture. Thus, while Erikson's (1963) idea that one cannot have a sense of identity outside of participation in some social group is still critically important, culture should not be understood as an add-on to personality that is derived from group membership. Rather, a personal identity is constructed out of culturally based experiences.

Such clients as those with psychotic or character-disordered diagnoses, who have poorly developed capacities to create meaning, often need considerable help in forming event representations and abstracting or confirming a sense of individual identity that can serve as a guide in social functioning. Since only life narratives that contain culturally validated content can be effective in negotiations with others, these individuals need help in understanding the content of culturally accepted meaning. Therefore, the clinical social worker is often a conveyor or representative of the culture as he or she helps the client understand what content is readily understood by others.

In accordance with Nelson's theory, however, culture enters meaning systems at two levels—as lexical/semantic structure and as event representations. Some clients have well-established event representations and have a sense of personal identity and experience but find that this personal identity and experience is degraded in the vocabulary of the lexical/semantic meaning system. Under these conditions it is difficult for the individual to maintain self-esteem because it is largely through the use of language that the individual can achieve a sense of participation in the larger human community and can, from an awareness of such participation, achieve validation of the importance of his or her own personal identity and the meaningfulness of his or her life.

Yet even more destructive to the functioning of the self is the situation in which there are no existing words within the communal language with which to capture that personal experience. When the linguistic forms utilized in the community do not provide the individual a means for expressing his or her own personal experience, the result can be a sense of identity fragmentation. This is essentially a socially imposed repression that may make persons doubt the accuracy of their sense of reality and ability to construct a personal identity.

This socially imposed repression of personal experience is, unfortunately, common for individuals who are members of minority groups in current Western societies where the language used by the community is determined primarily by a priviledged majority who may be quite ignorant of prominent characteristics of minority life. Another example of the manner in which the forms of expression available in the culture's linguistic system can become personally repressive involves the Freudian approach to femininity. Freud insisted both that sexuality was the bedrock of personality development and that sexuality was defined in terms of male experience. The adoption of this premise within a sexist culture and the elaboration of a language in which to describe personal experience that correlates only with male experience have led most feminists to conclude that the very concept of femininity in Western societies is elucive and difficult to define (Zaniardi, 1990). Periods of rapid social change often result in personal experiences for which there are no terms of expression; at such times there may be many people for whom the available verbal symbols have limited expressive capacity.

A tripartite comprehension of meaning, then, leads to the conclusion that a clinician must also have a tripartite concern about culture with a client. First, the client must be helped to form a personal sense of identity out of his or her own experiences in interpersonal interactions. The clinician must help the client contemplate and understand the nature of his or her experience within the contextual groups in which he or she has had in-person interactions. Such groups involve interaction in a variety of settings including school, work, and social situations. Of these groups, especially in the early childhood years, the family is clearly prominent, but this is not merely in terms of the intrapsychic features of individual family members. Nor is it merely in terms of the interpersonal relationships or structure of the family system. The client also needs to understand his or her experience in relation to the manner in which the individuals and the family group understand, convey, and participate in the culture of the larger social groups that surround them.

Second, assuming that the client has abstracted a personal identity out of experiences in interactions with others, the client needs to examine this identity in regard to its relative contribution to a narrative that may conceivably end in the achievement of his or her goals for the future. It is in this arena that the bulk of treatment literature has focused, since the client–therapist focus here is likely to be on dissatisfactions with experiences in interacting with others and on ways in which the client can alter those experiences in order to achieve increased effectiveness and self-esteem. Here, however, the client's evaluation of his or her personal identity must be seen as occurring in the framework of both the cultural context from which the foundation of event representations derive and the desired future goals. It is the importance of this framework and its influence on client–therapist negotiations that has all too often been neglected in clinical writing. Clinical social work's insistence on the importance of a person-in-situation perspective can be understood to include an assertion of the necessity of a cultural context for personal identity.

Although it is helpful for the therapist to be aware of major spheres of difference among groups, it is not possible for any clinician to be familiar in advance with all of the possible variations and permutations of a cultural/ethnic meaning system as this may be expressed in the unique families or communities encountered in practice. The therapist cannot know in advance what the client's experience has been and must rely on the client's ability to communicate this experience either through words or through actions within the treatment. However, the linguistic code shared by the broader community may, in fact, not include preexisting verbal symbols that can readily capture the experiences of some individuals. The clinician's third concern regarding culture, therefore, involves dealing with the relationship between the client's personal experiences and the symbols available in the broader culture.

There are critically important differences in the manner in which a therapist handles a situation in which a client encounters problems in expressing personal experience through the communally shared language. If the therapist uses the inadequate but available language to impose lexical/sematic meaning on the client's experience, the result will be repressive. On the other hand, the therapist can help the client recognize the frustration involved in not having a readily available symbolic vehicle for a legitimate personal experience and can join the client in a search for some appropriate way of capturing that experience. The client and therapist then normally find themselves creating a shared language within which the client's life experiences can be captured. The client may subsequently use this language to understand his or her personal identity when interacting in the larger social system. Under some circumstances either the client or the therapist may introduce the new symbolic vehicles to the culture beyond the treatment setting, thus leading to the possibility of changes in the culture of that broader community.

The Therapist's Responsibility for Content

The idea that psychotherapy is a science in which the therapist is a "blank screen" onto which the client projects feelings, thoughts, and behavior or in which there is some sort of universal inherited meaning has the advantage of allowing the therapist to evade any personal responsibility for the content of the meaning system that the client constructs in the treatment. On the other hand, if treatment is understood as an interpersonal process involving the creation of a narrated identity for the client, it is not possible for the therapist to avoid such responsibility. In fact, even if the therapist never makes any statement of belief during the course of a treatment enterprise, the content of the client's meaning system will still be influenced by the therapist's questions, which will have been formulated out of underlying theories and beliefs about treatment and human beings.

In the 1960s social workers had much optimism about the potential for changes in the structure of American society. At that time there was much criticism of individual treatment, including the assertion that "casework is dead." Clinicians felt very much on the defensive when it was asserted that treatment simply adjusted the individual to a sick society. Such a result was certainly not the clinicians' goal, nor was it their experience of what did occur in psychotherapy. Since that time it has been demonstrated that treatment can be effectively concluded on the basis of a variety of theoretical orientations but that the meaning system of the successfully treated client will invariably reflect the therapist's theoretical orientation.

A constructivist approach to knowledge, with its underlying comprehension of the fact that there is no such thing as ultimate, objective truth, indicates that therapists and clinical theorists, no matter how conscientious, are invariably participants in and constrained by the culture of their times. This premise seems evident in the fact that even someone like Freud, who was a genuine innovator and genius, could not and did not transcend some of the major prejudices common in his era. It is one of many fundamental paradoxes of existence that while human beings require some certainty about their understanding of the world in order to function, it is not possible for them to achieve truly certain and objective knowledge. Practicing clinical social workers need to be aware of this rather humbling situation.

At the same time, an awareness that total objective truth will always evade the therapist need not either preclude or detract from the practice of clinical social work. The ultimate goal of clinical treatment is improvement in the client's social functioning. Such improvement is ultimately accomplished, however, not by determining the specific behavior that is presumed to be more adaptive but, rather, by enabling individuals to understand more fully both themselves and the culture of the society in which they participate, so that they can make more informed choices about how they wish to act. In this context it is clear that the therapist does, at least at times, need to be a conveyor of the culture. Yet the therapist must also be able to allow the client to transcend culturally created meaning at times.

A demand that the therapist be able to transcend culturally created meaning is an impossible demand, one that none of us can ever completely achieve. Nevertheless, it places an understanding of the traditional requirement for self-awareness in the social worker in a somewhat different perspective. Self-awareness certainly includes an awareness of the meanings involved in one's own ethnic heritage as well as the honest and disciplined contemplation of the personal affective reactions engendered by interactions with clients (Devore & Schlessinger, 1987). However, it also includes some awareness of one's location within the history of the culture of the broader society, the relationship of this cultural meaning system to current economic and social structures, and the current tensions and influences for further change that may be operative.

In Gadamer's terms this would mean that the clinical social worker must consider his or her own "historicality" and must know how the world appears from that particular horizon. The social worker must have his or her own horizon before attempting to understand that of the client.

> But it is not the case that we acquire this horizon by placing ourselves within a historical situation. Rather, we must always already have a horizon in order to be able to place ourselves within a situation. For what do we mean by 'placing ourselves' in a situation? Certainly not just disregarding ourselves. This is necessary, of course, in that we must imagine the other situation. But into this other situation we must also bring ourselves.
>
> This placing of ourselves is not the empathy of one individual for another, nor is it the application to another person of our own criteria, but it always involves the attainment of a higher universality that overcomes, not only our own particularity, but also that of the other. . . . To acquire a horizon means that one learns to look beyond what is close at hand—not in order to look away from it, but to see it better within a larger whole and in truer proportion. (Gadamer, 1976, p. 131)

It seems unreasonably idealistic to believe that a clinical social worker can invariably achieve "a higher universality that overcomes," but perhaps this is a goal the social worker can strive for. Some years ago Stonequist (1937) developed the concept of marginality. This is the condition of a person who, having been exposed to at least two cultures, fully identified with neither. The marginal individual was considered to be vulnerable to personal conflict but also a potential agent for social change because of an ability to see beyond the meaning system of each culture. In negotiating therapeutic relationships with clients from a variety of cultural backgrounds, the clinical worker is, in fact, exposed to many cultures and perhaps can therefore be seen as a marginal person in Stonequist's terms. In the terms of the theory presented in this book, of course, it can be said that the clinical social worker should acquire identity complexity.

11 Constructing a Concordance

The primary activity of clinical treatment is the creation of a concordance, or therapeutic culture (Saari, 1986). In this endeavor the client practices the creation of meaning in collaboration with a therapist who diagnoses the capacity of the client's self to create meaning and then provides a relationship that will maximize that capacity. The assumption here is that the client will transfer the skills in the creation of meaning that have been learned, reorganized, or reaffirmed within the treatment relationship to interactions with other human beings outside the treatment itself. The content of the concordance is built so as to provide the client with an opportunity to internalize an identity that is both coherent and complex in order to maximize the possibilities for behavioral choice and adaptive social functioning.

The idea that the client and therapist together create a shared culture is perhaps not so very different from Winnicott's (1965) idea of the therapist providing a holding environment. Although Winnicott apparently did not make a point of saying that this holding environment was constructed, it seems consistent with his approach to treatment to think of the holding environment as being tailored specifically to the needs of the individual client and of its being interpersonally constructed by the client and the therapist in their interactions.

When treatment is understood in this manner, it becomes clear that it will never be possible to reduce its principles to a set of techniques to be followed. Indeed, this explains why prescriptions for clinical treatment cannot be derived in a simple fashion from symptom categories. This does not, however, mean that the clinical social worker does not use scientific theory in practice. In fact, this occurs in at least two different ways. First, as indicated in Chapter 8, studies of how the capacity to create meaning normally develops and evidence from studies of pathology provide guidelines for the clinician in how best to use his or her self, as well as other types of interventions, in a manner that will be growth-producing for the client. In addition, however, the therapist also uses theory as a framework within which the autobiographical story material is to be interpreted or understood.

Bruner (1983) has indicated that successful communication requires a shared and familiar context to aid the partners in making their communicative intentions clear to each other. The audience to whom a story is told, contrary to previous assumptions, does not merely play a passive role. There are prescriptions, which differ in various cultures, for how a listener is expected to behave. Such prescriptions usually include what sort of listener demeanor conveys respect for the storyteller, when and why the listener may interrupt, and how the audience conveys to the storyteller its level of admiration for or agreement with the story itself (Robinson, 1981). Polanyi (1979) has shown that the point of a story is often a matter of negotiation between the narrator and the listeners.

Certainly, it is true that a therapist is expected to listen attentively and purposefully, to indicate whether or not the points made by the client have been understood, and to request clarification if there is confusion. Since in order to be successful a communicative context must be cognitively and affectively manageable, the therapist must respond to the client in a manner that is consonant with what the client can comprehend and utilize. In addition, the manner in which the data of the client's story and the clinician's theoretical framework fit together is a matter of continual negotiation between the client and the therapist. It is through such negotiation that the content with which the client can alter his or her identity will be constructed.

The raw material on which the content of the concordance will be based comes from three sources. The first of these is the life story that the client tells in order to explain how his or her current state came about. Too often the therapeutic value of the client's simply telling his or her story is overlooked. Narration about oneself always involves the self in two different roles: narrator and protagonist. In telling stories about themselves, clients become actively engaged in separating the events of the story and their effects upon the protagonist from the attitude taken about those events by the narrator. The very act of constructing or telling an autobiographical story, therefore, automatically involves some observation or contemplation of the state of the self.

Since narrating does force contemplation, it helps the client obtain some psychological distance--or, to put this in more classical terms, it reinforces the functioning of an observing ego. In this sense, the very structure of self-narrative forces the creation of a psychological perspective involving motivations and intentions (Bruner & Lucariello, 1989). In other words, the structure of stories makes it necessary for the narrator to explain the inner worlds of the characters involved. In this way, telling one's life story requires the construction of a personal identity.

In addition to requiring the construction of a psychological world, narrative structure enables problem solving. Feldman (1989) has indicated that because of the two perspectives involved, the telling of stories makes possible the reflective activities of analysis and later of invention. It is through these cognitive processes that the person can search for potential strategies for dealing with life and determining the most attractive choices. Such problem solving is, of course, at the heart of therapy. Narrative structure can be seen to underlie dreams, fantasies, and play, all of which have been recognized as productive arenas for therapeutic work.

The second source of the raw material for the content of the concordance comes from new data about the client that emerge in the course of client–therapist interactions. As Schafer (1980) observed, clients "show" as well as tell about themselves:

> If we are forever telling stories about ourselves and others and to ourselves and others, it must be added that people do more than tell: like authors, they also show. As there is no hard-and-fast line between telling and showing, either in literary narrative or in psychoanalysis, the competent psychoanalyst deals with telling as a form of showing and with showing as a form of telling. Everything in analysis is both communication and demonstration. (p. 38)

Not all of that what is meaningful to any individual is available in a conscious meaning system. Indeed, much of what affects human beings the most is recorded in action patterns that are not verbally accessible. These can be available for contemplation and understanding only if they are first concretized through action in some form (Saari, 1986).

In much of current clinical theory repetition compulsion is now considered to be one form in which human beings attempt to master difficult situations from the past through acting them out in the present (Basch, 1988). The acting out of aspects of past difficulties is, therefore, one of the common explanations for transference phenomena. Interpreting the transference can be understood simply as the clinician's helping the client recognize and put into words what the client has been demonstrating through actions. It is also common for clients to find themselves quite surprised at what they actually articulate in therapy. It must be kept in mind that the client's story telling is itself a form of action.

Interestingly, Krystal (1988) and Horowitz (1972) have both suggested that there may be at least five different levels of consciousness and that in order to remember something that has occurred in the past, one may need to get into that level of consciousness. Therefore, the client's ability to demonstrate aspects of his meaning may at times depend on the psychological state that is evoked in the client–therapist interactions as well as on concurrent actions. Moreover, some of what has been considered to be transference may be the client's attempts to reach a certain level of consciousness or state of mind within which the encoded meaning from the past may be accessible.

The therapist's explanatory perspective provides the third source of raw material for the content of the concordance. Since it is not possible for the therapist's own meaning system to have no effect on the client's meaning system, it is hoped that the clinician will utilize only the most recent and reliable scientific information in an explanation for a client. Certainly, it is important for clinicians to remain current in regard to evolving theoretical explanations. However, clinical treatment must be seen as distinctly different from pure education, in which the focus is on conveying and evaluating currently accepted theory. In therapy the goal is to articulate in lexical/semantic terms an explanation that will fit with the client's personal experience at the conceptual level.

No doubt all clinicians automatically use with clients some of the technical terms from their theoretical understanding. There are some clients, probably themselves professionals, for whom more of the scientifically understood language will be useful in capturing personal experience. However, for many clients professional jargon is cumbersome and distracting. For these clients, theoretical concepts can be expressed through language selected from the entire range of culturally available terms--from everyday experiences, literature, art, soap opera or other television programming, and so forth. In short, analogies can be and should be drawn from the sources with which the particular client is most familiar.

The causal propositions in the concordance, as in the client's identity, do not have scientific status. Nevertheless, for these to have maximal effectiveness they should be logically plausible, have internal coherence, and be consonant with whatever confirmable facts are known about the client's life. It is generally useful for the clinician to use current psychological theory as a guideline in the construction of the concordance even if the words utilized are selected from some other field of experience or endeavor.

If, however, the goal for the client is improvement in social functioning, the terms used to describe the client's identity (and therefore of the concordance from which this is selected) must be those that can be comprehended within the social order in which the client wishes to participate. That is,

> life stories must mesh, so to speak, within a community of life stories; tellers and listeners must share some "deep structure" about the nature of a "life," for if the rules of life-telling are altogether arbitrary, tellers and listeners will surely be alienated by a failure to grasp what the other is saying or what he thinks the other is hearing. (Bruner, 1987, p. 21)

The psychologically minded preoccupations of current Western societies, institutionalized through phenomena like television talk shows, generally mean that new theories of human behavior quickly become expressed in or absorbed by popularized psychological explanations. For this reason, there is often some similarity between the client's language forms, which have been derived from the general culture, and the language forms utilized by the therapist, which have presumably been derived from the professional or scientific culture.

Creating Identity Complexity

Bruner (1987) has pointed out that any story is better understood by understanding alternative ways in which it can be told. In a similar vein, Schafer (1980) has indicated that psychoanalysis involves the retelling of a life story:

> From the acceptance of this new account, there follows a systematic project of constructing a psychoanalytic reality in which one retells the past and the present, the infantile and the adult, the imagined and the so-called real, and the analytic relationship and all

other significant relationships. One retells all this in terms that are increasingly focused and coordinated in psychoanalytic terms of action. One achieves a narrative redescription of reality. This retelling is adapted to the clinical context and relationship, the purpose of which is to understand anew the life and the problems in question. The analysand joins in the retelling (redescribing, reinterpreting) as the analysis progresses. The second reality becomes a joint enterprise and a joint experience. (p. 50)

This retelling of stories plays a central role in the way in which therapy helps a client move toward the achievement of identity complexity. Certainly, in work with clients with severe deficits in the capacity to create meaning, the ability to retain one meaning must be attained prior to work on complexity. However, understanding more detail about how treatment can help the appropriate client achieve identity complexity is very important.

Identity and the concordance are both meaning systems; it may not be excessively redundant to point out here that meaning is necessarily context dependent (Mishler, 1979). Individuals who wish to function in modern societies need the ability to function in a variety of different cultural contexts. The ability of an individual to understand or to tell his or her own life story in a manner that is consonant with a variety of contexts ought to lead to a greater potential for healthy adaptive behavior. In fact, it may well be that one of the common characteristics of psychological pathology is the inability to retain a sense of meaning when moving from one context to another. Certainly, the inability to maintain a sense of self-esteem when moving from one context to another is common.

A clinician's ability to "transcontext" meaning becomes very important for the conduct of the treatment. For example, one common cognitive activity of the therapist is to listen to the client's story with an ear toward how the action and events of the story might have been viewed from the perspective of one of the other characters in the story. The therapist might then decide to share the view achieved in this manner directly with the client, but regardless of what is done with that information, the therapist has achieved a better understanding of the client's situation. The process of achieving this different perspective is essentially that of "transcontexting."

Another way in which the clinician often utilizes the ability to transcontext is in the imagination of the future. One of the fundamental reasons that people seek therapy is their inability to imagine themselves in a future in which personal goals have been achieved. Parents like those of the child Emily (see Chapter 5) have a special need to talk about what will occur in the future when putting the child to sleep. In all probability, such discussion of the future contributes to a sense of comfortable continuity in the child, something like Winnicott's (1956) "going on being." In a similar sense, envisioning the client's ability to function more adequately in some future context may be a special therapeutic function (Loewald, 1960). If the therapist then relates to the client as someone who is capable of achieving that future, the client may gradually adopt some of that perspective for himself or herself.

Daniel Stern (1985) has proposed that affect attunement and intersubjectivity basically involve cross-modal matching, that is, the matching of another's vitality affect in another form that is experienced as empathic. Such cross-modal matching can, however, be seen simply as transcontexting. Such a viewpoint seems to make considerable sense out of some aspects of traditional clinical theory. For example, much of what has been called verbal "interpretation" in treatment is simply the act of reframing what the client has already conveyed into other words; such interpretations might be called cross-verbal matching.

If Stern is correct in the implication that only experiences that have been affectively attuned can become conscious, then affectively attuned transcontexting in clinical treatment can be understood to make conscious what was previously unconscious. Freud may have seen the mechanism of making conscious what was unconscious as a means of uncovering biologically inherited meaning. Another way, however, of viewing the value of creating a new consciousness where this did not exist previously involves an understanding of the coexistence of multiple meanings and the adaptive potential of a complex identity.

Another means through which interpretation has been considered to be effective is metaphor (Ekstein, 1983; Siegelman, 1990). Metaphor expands the connections between contexts. Nelson's theory of meaning helps to explain the way in which metaphor probably functions. A metaphor can be understood to be a word that occupies a particular slot in and is abstracted from one event representation and is then placed within another event representation. In this manner the single word serves as a connection for the particular individual between two event representations and all of the associated meanings involved with each. For example, a client who had lost his mother through death remarked that when sitting in the waiting room he felt the burden of the therapy wrapped around him like a shroud. Through the metaphor of the shroud he had made a connection between his experience of his mother and her death, and his therapy with the female therapist.

Rothenberg (1988) has studied creativity in both the arts and psychotherapy and has specified some additional ways of expanding meaning. He believes that the articulation of error is one means of creating new meaning, an idea that may hark back to Freud's notions of parapraxes. For example, at another time the aforementioned client referred to his therapist using his former wife's first name. Focusing in treatment on the expansion of such errors and on their potential meaning is another way of helping clients achieve new perspectives on their own experiences.

Rothenberg considers metaphors to be examples of what he calls the "homospatial process," in which multiple discrete entities are brought into the same space. He has described another process, which he terms "Janusian," in which simultaneous opposites and antitheses are utilized as the matrix of a problem. Clinical examples of the Janusian process abound in attempts at getting clients to recognize ambivalence and conflicting feelings about the significant people and events in their lives.

It is likely that there are many other ways in which clinicians use cognitive processes and skills in the creation of complexity in a concordance. Most of these ways of dealing with clinical material have been utilized from the early days of client-therapist interactions. It is important, however, to recognize that these are used as a means of achieving another perspective on the client's story rather than as a means of achieving a perspective that somehow captures the "accurate" version of the story or the ultimate "truth."

Conceptions of Therapeutic Interaction

The failure in traditional clinical theory to allow for the possibility of multiple truths, in combination with insufficient emphasis on the degree to which treatment is dependent upon the interpersonal interactions of which it is composed, has led to some unnecessary confusion about the nature of the interactions within a therapeutic relationship. This is evident, for example, in the often raised question as to whether the relationship is "real" or "transferential." In a broad sense, transference has generally been defined as the effect of the client's past experiences on the relationship with the therapist. To the extent that the client's reactions to the therapist were due to previous experiences rather than to the therapist, the relationship was not considered "real."

Freud (1905) originally identified transference in his unsuccessful work with Dora and initially saw it as a hindrance to therapy. Later, however, it was believed central to treatment effectiveness; that is, transference was understood to be a distorted view of the therapist, who was seen as attempting to help the patient through the objective application of scientific truth. The distortions that the patient introduced into the treatment relationship were thought to reflect the distortions in the patient's view of the world. If these distortions could be resolved or worked through with the patient, thereby achieving an accurate picture of the therapist, the patient would be cured.

A more current perspective would, of course, acknowledge both that there is no single truth about the nature of the client–therapist relationship and that there is considerable question about any therapist's ability to be truly objective about interactions in which he or she is a participant. If it is understood that the content of the concordance is not unassailable truth but, rather, an attempt at moving the client toward identity complexity, then it becomes unnecessary for the therapist to be scientifically objective or omniscient or infallible. That the therapist may not agree with the client's point of view does not necessarily indicate that the therapist's view is the correct one and that the client's is pathologically distorted. Instead, it simply provides an example of the differing perspectives that must be taken into account in human interactions. Only if the participants of an interaction explain their perspectives to each other can it be determined if one perspective is more persuasive than the other. Usually, of course, a number of perspectives have validity and can be allowed to coexist.

Once it is understood that a relationship by definition involves the meaning attributed to an interaction, the question of whether the therapeutic relationship is transferential or real becomes an irrelevant one. As Loewald (1960) pointed out, if transference is understood to be the meaning attributed to an interpersonal interaction, then it is clear that transference is present in all human relationships and is the very element that gives them their importance. Furthermore, all human meaning is constructed within the framework of the individual's previous experiences and separating the influence of the past from that of the present in regard to meaning content is not an easy matter.

Nevertheless, transference in the sense of the meaning the client assigns to the therapeutic relationship is extremely important, since it does provide an example, often an affectively intense one, of the content and process involved in the client's construction of meaning within a human interaction. Within the treatment situation the only thing that the two (or more) participants have directly experienced together involves the therapy-related interactions between them. Attempts at understanding how these same interactions have been differentially experienced helps to highlight how the client constructs meaning, the possibilities of legitimate alternative views, and the content that is shared by the participants.

Unless the client and therapist have a shared purpose, a shared understanding about interactive roles and procedures, and some minimum of shared content, the treatment will not proceed well. In treatment, as in any other human interaction, the level of agreement between the participants needs to be periodically reexamined in order to reestablish what is shared. Traditional clinical theory has, of course, recognized this need for shared understanding, which has often been referred to as the "working alliance." There have sometimes been implications that the therapist–client relationship in the working alliance is somehow more real than in the transference. Such a formulation might work in a purely abstract sense, but in practice any clinician knows that the client's meaning does not segment itself in this manner.

Client–therapist interactions are real in the sense that there should be nothing in the least ephemeral or mysterious about them; they are genuine interactions between two human beings. In fact, it is the very real quality of all the client–therapist interactions, regardless of the content discussed, that makes a working alliance possible. Constructivist approaches to knowledge normally emphasize differences in perspective, that is, that the ideas created by two individuals who experience the same event will inevitably have some differences about the nature and significance of that event. While this is the case, it must also be emphasized that shared meaning is possible specifically because when two individuals do participate in the same event, there are shared elements around which there can be agreement. The exploration of divergent perspectives can only become a constructive activity when there is a background of shared experience.

In treatment, of course, the frequency and manner in which the sharing of content and the examination of the interpersonal interactions within the treatment setting occur depend largely upon the state of the client's self and the relative amount of interpsychic space needed to maximize client functioning. For this reason a therapist needs to pay minute-to-minute attention to both the degree of shared content and the extent of interpsychic space. What this means is that the therapist must be flexible about the manner in which he or she interacts, gearing the handling of all encounters as closely as possible to the needs of the client.

There are at least three other ways in which traditional theory has implied that client–therapist interactions are not "real," thereby undermining an understanding of this endeavor from a truly interpersonal point of view. The first is the implication that the client–therapist relationship is not real because it is not a part of the client's everyday life. The purpose of therapy is to provide the client with a place within which to step back from everyday life in order to contemplate it and thus achieve increased mastery over it through an imposed psychological distance. Since a clinician's involvement in the client's life in some role other than that of therapist would diminish the clinician's ability to take and encourage a contemplative rather than an activity-oriented stance toward problem solving, it is normally best for a clinician to interact with the client only in the role of a therapist. It would seem, however, to make more sense to refer to the therapeutic situation as one in which the therapist retains boundaries around the role he or she plays in the client's life rather than to indicate that the relationship is not real.

The second way in which the client–therapist relationship has been considered to be other than real is its presumed tendency to induce regression to an earlier stage of development. Such a notion is based on the theoretical understanding that psychotherapy works by having the client return to the developmental stage at which the presumed psychic deficit occurred, in order for the therapy to repair it. This formulation utilizes both a fundamentally linear conception of causation and the notion that treatment works through the reversal of the cause of the problem.

From the point of view regarding treatment offered here, it seems reasonable to assume that the context of therapy should be designed so as to maximize the clinician's ability to diagnose the client's capacity to create meaning as well as to maximize the client's ability to develop that capacity further. There is no reason to believe that clients return to an earlier life stage in treatment, nor is it desirable that they should do so. Instead, clients demonstrate within the context designed for treatment the level of their current capacity to create meaning (Gill, 1982).

Modell (1988, 1990), who does not think the treatment relationship should be thought of as regressive, has indicated that it is asymmetrical in relation to authority. That is the third sense in which client–therapist treatment interactions are considered by some to be not "real." There seems, however, to be something strange about saying a relationship is not real when what one means is that the participants have assumed different roles that also have different degrees of expertise or authority. A student–teacher relationship, for example, also involves roles with an unequal distribution of expertise and authority, but it would strike most people as rather odd to refer to this relationship as not real for that reason. Thus, it does not seem to be particularly useful to think of the client–therapist relationship as other than real.

Particularly in recent years there have been numerous formulations about transference and countertransference, both of which have sometimes been seen as helpful and at other times as a hindrance to the therapeutic work (Geddes & Pajik, 1990; Grayer & Sax, 1986). Even granting that there is a wide range of ways in which clients and therapists can experience each other, at times the detail of these formulations has become almost more confusing than useful. Clearly, to the extent to which the meaning involved in transference and countertransference can be used to promote the concordance and its usable complexity, treatment is promoted. On the other hand, to the extent that the meaning of the interactions constructed by either participant threatens the essential minimum of shared meaning and a working alliance, that meaning is a hindrance. It is likely, however, that most often the cause of unmanageable transference and/or countertransference can be located in problems in the modulation of the interpsychic space required for the functioning of the self of either or both participants.

Projective identification, a concept with roots in Klein's work, has become a popular means of describing the interactional dynamics in therapy (Ogden, 1982). While this concept has certainly been a useful approach to the nature of such interactions, the theoretical formulations underneath it seem unnecessarily complicated in the supposition of projections, introjections and identifications, to say nothing of "part-objects." Interactional dynamics can be made simpler by an approach in which it is understood that just as individuals construct an identity for themselves, so also do they construct the identity of the other person with whom they interact.

Since the characteristics that are attributed to any person with whom the individual is interacting in the present are derived from the individual's past experiences, it is inevitable that there will be some sort of emotional identification or involvement with those characteristics; this occurs, of course, in all relationships. It becomes a problem when the experience on which the attributed quality is based was extremely negative or when the individual's meaning system is so unstable that the existence of the attributed quality must be rigidly maintained while the possibility of other qualities is denied. An investigation of the identity that the client constructs for the therapist is, therefore, necessary for an understanding of what the client expects other human beings to be like.

Meaning is, of course, not always consciously constructed but, instead, may be enacted through the interactions with the therapist. It seems to be the case that there is a tendency for human beings to behave interactively as if they did, in fact, have the qualities that have been attributed to them by the interactional partner. This dynamic is useful in helping clients become the more competent persons the therapist envisions them to be in the future. However, it also means that a therapist can sometimes act as if he or she has qualities, often negative ones, that may have been unconsciously attributed to him or her by the client.

Since the purpose of therapy is the examination and construction of the client's meaning system, the therapist's actions should be geared to promote this purpose. Therefore, when therapists discover themselves acting in ways that are not compatible with their professional identity and the goals of the treatment, they should seek an understanding of what influences may be contributing to such activity. Often this may lead to a new understanding about the client's unconscious. On the other hand, of course, therapists must also consider the possibility that there is something about the client that has elicited some aspect of a not yet constructed meaning from their own past experiences.

In a work on transference and countertransference that is now considered a classic, Racker (1968) called attention to the fact that the therapist could react to the client through an identification with the client or through an identification with some person who had been a significant other in the client's life. In fact, because both the client and the therapist simultaneously construct both their own and each other's identities within the treatment, both persons can act out the relational attributes of a whole host of people over the course of a treatment endeavor.

Loewald (1975) described the treatment process through the wonderful analogy of the play. The patient is the author, the therapist the stage director. Both patient and therapist, at various times, act out the parts of the many characters in the patient's play. It is essential, however, for the therapist to stop the action periodically in order to reflect on its implications. In this way, the therapist is also a drama critic and increasingly engages the patient in becoming one as well. Over the course of the action and interpretation of its meaning, therefore, the play is rewritten many times.

A clinical social worker should never forget, however, that the content of the play as it is being rewritten is heavily influenced by the quality of the client's experience within the treatment itself. The content at any given moment must be examined for the way in which it is reflecting the client's current experience of the social worker, for, in the long run, the content of the client's identity will reflect the nature of the relationship with the social worker. It is for this reason that Schafer (1983) has commented that the history in which the therapist can have the most confidence is the story of the unfolding of the treatment itself.

IV CONCLUSION

12 Relationship Revisited

The most enduring concept in clinical social work's treatment theory has been that of the relationship between client and social worker, which Biestek (1957) described as the soul of social casework. Yet in the past, understanding of precisely how a professional relationship is therapeutic was limited. Recent advances in research and practice experience now make it possible to create more specific conceptualizations of the manner in which a relationship can be differentially utilized to assist a variety of individuals in maintaining and developing further the capacities that underlie psychological health and adaptive social functioning. The formulation that has been put forth in this book is only one way of understanding the therapeutic effects of relationships. It is in many ways a new and untested conceptualization that will need further investigation through both practice experience and formal research. Whatever the long-range viability of the specifics of this formulation should turn out to be, however, the availability of these ideas is an indication that understanding the nature of therapeutic interactions is now possible in much more depth than has previously been the case. Even if the ideas proposed here eventually prove to be woefully inadequate, others can be found to refine or replace them.

Since in actual practice it is impossible to separate out content and process, the attempt to do so here undoubtedly has some drawbacks. At the same time, it has appeared that, at present, conceptualizing treatment requires an understanding of both these elements and that the conceptualizing could not proceed without an attempt at explicating their different properties and effects. The interrelationships between content and process, between causal

factors and interpretation in treatment, is complex and will undoubtedly need more complete explication than has been possible
here. Separating out these elements for consideration, however, as
well as understanding that there are differences between meaning,
motivation, and causation, promises to provide a much more adequate framework for research into practice.

Unfortunately, to date too much of practice research has attempted to view treatment exclusively from a perspective of causal
analysis within which the elements of meaning are inevitably neglected. Currently, there is a growing interest among researchers in
narrative and other types of content analysis, which may prove to
be productive in elucidating the manner in which identity is built
and/or supplemented within treatment. It will be important, however, not to abandon causal theory in examining practice. The
manner in which the capacity to create meaning functions and
develops, both over the course of the normal life span and in the
treatment enterprise, needs much further understanding. This will
require a causal, developmental theoretical framework.

Unfortunately for many years the psychoanalytic discipline, presumably out of a continuation of Freud's fear of criticism from the
uninitiated, maintained the position that valid psychoanalytic
knowledge could come only from observations of the psychoanalytic treatment situation itself, a position that has discouraged the
development of research into the propositions upon which psychoanalytic treatment rests. Currently, there are many psychoanalysts
who do not agree with this position (see, for example, Eagle, 1987).
In fact, as is evidenced in the work of Mahler, Stern, Bruner, Emde,
and a number of others, the most important advances in knowledge about human functioning in recent years seem to have come
primarily from research on psychodynamic theories conducted
outside the treatment situation. There is now a need not only to
continue this research but also to test out its applicability within
the context of treatment.

In dealing with research focused on the treatment situation and
the interactions within it, however, it is important to keep in mind
Nelson's (1989b) finding that the preschooler Emily (see Chapter 5)
used much of her time alone to organize her perceptions of the
world and to form a representational world. In a similar sense,
much of the work that a client must do in order to benefit from
treatment may occur not during the sessions but between them.
For this reason it may be advisable not to limit conceptualizations
of therapeutic effectiveness to the immediate interactions within
the treatment setting itself.

For many years now clinical social work has been facing the dilemma that any framework for understanding treatment seemed to involve a content focus that was fundamentally ethnocentric. Attempts at avoiding this problem seemed to imply the necessity of a theory that involved a sterile scientism in which neither values nor a truly human interaction could be encompassed. Understanding that mental health involves identity complexity and the development of the capacity to create meaning appears to provide a fruitful way of dealing with this dilemma and can also provide the clinician with some guidelines for setting goals within treatment. This concept of mental health, however, requires much further examination.

The notion of event representations and Nelson's tripartite theory of meaning are conceptual developments with major implications for clinical social work. While research now implies that the infant has available perceptual information at a much earlier age than was previously thought possible (Mandler, 1990), the idea that the structures for processing this information are achieved through social participation is highly compatible with social work's traditional perspective. It would seem that this theory has the potential for providing more adequate explanations for the relationship between culture and personality and between social organization and individual pathology than any previously available theory.

Separating the capacity to create meaning from the content of identity, as well as understanding that all human interactional situations involve both a social structure and a culture, seems to have the potential for shedding light on some intraprofessional arguments about the nature of the causes of individual pathology. Clearly, the full development of the capacity to create meaning requires access to full participation within social structures. When justice and equality do not prevail, poverty, discrimination, and oppression have malignant effects on individuals. Treatment interventions with individuals will never obviate the need to create a more equitable society. However, an increased ability to explicate the causal links between social dysfunctions and individual pathology should lead not only to better clinical treatment but also to more persuasive documentation on which to base appeals for changes in the social system.

This is an exciting time for those interested in clinical social work theory. There are myriad opportunities for further understanding.

References

Agar, M., & Hobbs, J. R. (1982). Interpreting discourse: Coherence and analysis of ethnographic interviews. *Discourse Processes, 5,* 1–32.

Ainsworth, M. D. S., Blehar, M. C., Waters, E., & Wall, S. (1978). *Patterns of attachment.* Hillsdale, NJ: Erlbaum.

Allen, V. L., Wilder, D. A., & Atkinson, M. L. (1983). Multiple group membership and social identity. In T. R. Sarbin & K. E. Scheibe (Eds.), *Studies in social identity* (pp. 92–115). New York: Praeger.

Baldwin, J. M. (1902). *Social and ethical interpretations in mental development.* New York: Macmillan.

Basch, M. F. (1976). The concept of affect: A re-examination. *Journal of the American Psychoanalytic Association, 24*(4), 759–777.

Basch, M. F. (1988). *Understanding psychotherapy: The science behind the art.* New York: Basic Books.

Becker, H. S. (1986). Culture: A sociological view. *Doing things together: Selected papers.* Evanston, IL: Northwestern University Press, pp. 11–24.

Behrends, R. S., & Blatt, S. J. (1985). Internalization and psychological development throughout the life cycle. *The Psychoanalytic Study of the Child, 40,* 11–39.

Bettelheim, B. (1976). *The uses of enchantment: The meaning and importance of fairy tales.* New York: Knopf.

Biestek, F. P. (1957). *The casework relationship.* Chicago: Loyola University Press.

Blanck, G., & Blanck, R. (1974). *Ego psychology: Theory and practice.* New York: Columbia University Press.

Blanck, G., & Blanck, R. (1977). The transference object and the real object. *International Journal of Psychoanalysis, 58,* 33–44.

Blatt, S. J., & Wild, C. M. (1976). *Schizophrenia: A developmental approach.* New York: Academic Press.

Bollas, C. (1983). Expressive uses of countertransference. *Contemporary Psychoanalysis, 19,* 1–33

Bowlby, J. (1969). *Attachment and loss* (Vol. 1). New York: Basic Books.

Bronowski, J. (1978). *The common sense of science.* Cambridge, MA: Harvard University Press.

Bruch, H. (1969). Hunger and instinct. *Journal of Nervous and Mental Disorders, 149,* 91–144.

Bruner, J. S. (1983). *Child's talk: Learning to use language.* New York: Norton.

Bruner, J. S. (1986). *Actual minds, possible worlds.* Cambridge, MA: Harvard University Press.

Bruner, J. S. (1987). Life as narrative. *Social Research, 54,* 11–32.

Bruner, J. S., & Lucariello, J. (1989). *Narratives from the crib.* Cambridge, MA: Harvard University Press.

Bruner, J. S., Olver, R. R., & Greenfield, P. M. (1966). *Studies in cognitive growth.* New York: Wiley.

Burke, K. (1945). *The grammar of motives.* New York: Prentice-Hall.

Chestang, L. W. (1979). Competencies and knowledge in clinical social work: A dual perspective. In P. L. Ewalt (Ed.), *Toward a definition of clinical social work* (pp. 1–12). Washington, DC: National Association of Social Workers.

Coddington, R. D., & Bruch, H. (1970). Gastric perceptivity in normal, obese, and schizophrenic subjects. *Psychosomatics, 11,* 571–579.

Cofer, C. N. (1977). On the constructive theory of memory. In F. Weizmann & I. C. Uzgiris (Eds.), *The structuring of experience* (pp. 319–341). New York: Plenum Press.

Cohler, B. J. (1982). Personal narrative and life course. In P. B. Baltes & O. G. Brim (Eds.), *Life-span development and behavior* (Vol. 4, pp. 206–241). New York: Academic Press.

Comas-Diaz, L., & Griffith, E. E. H. (1988). Introduction: On culture and psychotherapeutic care. In L. Comas-Diaz & E. E. H. Griffith (Eds.), *Clinical guidelines in cross-cultural mental health* (pp. 1–5). New York: Wiley.

Cooley, C. H. (1964). *Human nature and the social order.* New York: Schoken Books.

Darwin, C. (1872). *The expression of emotions in man and animals.* Chicago: University of Chicago Press.

Demos, E. V. (1982). Affect in early infancy. *Psychoanalytic Inquiry, 1,* 533–575.

Devore, W., & Schlessinger, E. G. (1987). *Ethnic-sensitive social work practice.* Columbus, OH: Merrill.

Donaldson, M. (1978). *Children's minds.* New York: Norton.

Draper, B. J. (1979). Black language as an adaptive response to a hostile environment. In C. B. Germaine (Ed.), *Social work practice: People and environments* (pp. 267–281). New York: Columbia University Press.

Eagle, M. N. (1987). *Recent developments in psychoanalysis: A critical review.* Cambridge, MA: Harvard University Press.

Eissler, K. R. (1952). Remarks on the psychotherapy of schizophrenia. In E. B. Brody & F. C. Redlich (Eds.), *Psychotherapy with schizophrenics* (pp. 130–167). New York: International Universities Press.

Ekstein, R. (1983). *Children of time and space, of action and impulse.* New York: Aronson.

Emde, R. N. (1981). Changing models of infancy and the nature of early development: Remodeling the foundation. *Journal of the American Psychoanalytic Association, 29,* 177–220.

Emde, R. N. (1989). The infant's relationship experience: Developmental and affective aspects. In A. J. Sameroff & R. N. Emde (Eds.), *Relationship disturbances in early childhood: A developmental approach* (pp. 33–52). New York: Basic Books.

Erikson, E. H. (1958). *Young man Luther.* New York: Norton.

Erikson, E. H. (1963). *Childhood and society* (2nd ed.). New York: Norton.

Erikson, E. H. (1969). *Gandhi's truth.* New York: Norton.

Erikson, E. H. (1980). *Identity and the life cycle.* New York: Norton.

Feldman, C. F. (1989). Problem-solving narratives. In K. Nelson (Ed.), *Narratives from the crib* (pp. 98–119). Cambridge, MA: Harvard University Press.

Freud, S. (1900). The interpretation of dreams. *The standard edition of the complete psychological works of Sigmund Freud* (Vols. 4 and 5). London: Hogarth Press.

Freud, S. (1905). Fragment of an analysis of a case of hysteria. *The standard edition of the complete psychological works of Sigmund Freud* (Vol. 7, pp. 1–122). London: Hogarth Press, 1953.

Freud, S. (1915). The unconscious. *The standard edition of the complete psychological works of Sigmund Freud* (Vol. 14, pp. 166–204). London: Hogarth Press, 1957.

Freud, S. (1917). Mourning and melancholia. *The standard edition of the complete psychological works of Sigmund Freud* (Vol. 14, pp. 237–260). London: Hogarth Press, 1957.

Freud, S. (1920). Beyond the pleasure principle. *The standard edition of the complete psychological works of Sigmund Freud* (Vol. 18, pp. 7–64). London: Hogarth Press, 1955.

Freud, S. (1923). The ego and the id. *The standard edition of the complete psychological works of Sigmund Freud* (Vol. 19, pp. 3–66). London: Hogarth Press, 1961.

Gadamer, H. (1976). The historicity of understanding. In P. Connerton (Ed.), *Critical sociology: Selected readings* (pp. 104–133). New York: Penguin Books.

Gay, P. (1988). *Freud: A life for our time.* New York: Norton.

Geddes, M. J., & Pajik, A. K. (1990). A multidimensional typology of countertransference responses. *Clinical Social Work Journal, 18,* 257–272.

Gergen, K. J. (1989). Warranting voice and the elaboration of self. In J. Shotter & K. J. Gergen (Eds.), *Tests of identity* (pp. 70–81). London: Sage.

Gergen, K. J., & Gergen, M. M. (1983). Narratives of self. In T. R. Sarbin & K. E. Scheibe (Eds.), *Studies in social identity* (pp. 254–273). New York: Praeger.

Gergen, K. J., & Gergen, M. M. (1987). The self in temporal perspective. In R. P. Abeles (Ed.), *Life-span perspectives and social psychology* (pp. 121–137). Hillsdale, NJ: Erlbaum.

Gill, M. M. (1982). *Analysis of transference: Vol. I. Theory and technique.* New York: International Universities Press.

Goldberg, A. (1988). *A fresh look at psychoanalysis: The view from self psychology.* Hillsdale, NJ: The Analytic Press.

Grayer, E., & Sax, P. (1986). A model for the diagnostic and therapeutic use of countertransference. *Clinical Social Work Journal, 14,* 295–309.

Greenberg, J. A., & Mitchell, S. A. (1983). *Object relations in psychoanalytic theory.* Cambridge, MA: Harvard University Press.

Guidano, V. F. (1987). *The complexity of the self: A developmental guide to psychopathology and therapy.* New York: Guilford Press.

Hartman, A. (1988). Foreword. In R. A. Dorfman (Ed.), *Paradigms of clinical social work* (pp. vii–xi). New York: Bruner/Mazel.

Hartmann, H. (1958). *Ego psychology and the problem of adaptation* (D. Rapaport, Trans.). New York: International Universities Press.

Hartmann, H., & Loewenstein, R. M. (1962). Notes on the superego. *The Psychoanalytic Study of the Child, 17,* 42–81.

Hebb, D. O. (1949). *The organization of behavior.* New York: Wiley.

Heidegger, M. (1927). *Being and time.* (J. Macquarrie & E. Robinson, Trans.). New York: Harper & Row, 1962.

Holt, R. W. (1976). Drive as wish. A reconsideration of the psychoanalytic theory of motivation. In M. M. Gill & P. S. Holzman (Eds.), *Psychology versus metapsychology: Psychoanalytic essays in honor of George S. Klein* (*Psychological Issues,* Monograph 36). New York: International Universities Press.

Horowitz, M. J. (1972). Modes of representation of thought. *Journal of the American Psychoanalytic Association, 20,* 793–819.

Hunter, K. M. (1989). A science of individuals: Medicine and casuistry. *Journal of Medicine and Philosophy, 14,* 193–212.

Imre, R. M. (1982). *Knowing and caring: Philosophical issues in social work.* New York: University Press of America.

Izard, C. E. (1977). *Human emotions.* New York: Plenum.

Jacobson, E. (1964). *The self and the object world.* New York: International Universities Press.

Jalali, B. (1988). Ethnicity, cultural adjustment, and behavior: Implications for family therapy. In L. Comas-Diaz & E. E. H. Griffith (Eds.), *Clinical guidelines in cross-cultural mental health* (pp. 9–32). New York: Wiley.

Kagan, J. (1981). *The second year of life: The emergence of self.* Cambridge, MA: Harvard University Press.

Kernberg, O. F. (1975). *Borderline conditions and pathological narcissism.* New York: Aronson.

Klein, G. S. (1976). *Psychoanalytic theory.* New York: International Universities Press.

Klein, M. (1952). In J. Rivere (Ed.), *Developments in psychoanalysis.* London: Hogarth Press.

Klein, M. (1964). *Contributions to psychoanalysis, 1921–1945.* New York: McGraw-Hill.

Kohut, H. (1971). *The analysis of the self.* New York: International Universities Press.

Kohut, H. (1984). *How does analysis cure?* Chicago: University of Chicago Press.

Krystal, H. (1988). *Integration and self-healing: Affect, trauma and alexithymia.* New York: The Analytic Press.

Kuhn, T. S. (1970). *The structure of scientific revolutions.* Chicago: University of Chicago Press.

Labov, W. (1972). *Language in the inner city: Studies in the black English vernacular.* Philadelphia: University of Pennsylvania Press.

Lacan, J. (1973). *The four fundamental concepts of psychoanalysis.* New York: Norton.

Langs, R. (1979). *The therapeutic environment.* New York: Aronson.

Lewis, M., & Brooks-Gunn, J. (1979). *Social cognition and the acquisition of self.* New York: Plenum.

Lichtenberg, J. D. (1983). *Psychoanalysis and infant research.* Hillsdale, NJ: The Analytic Press.

Lichtenberg, J. D. (1989). *Psychoanalysis and motivation.* Hillsdale, NJ: The Analytic Press.

Lichtenberg, J., Bornstein, M., & Silver, D. (Eds.). (1984). *Empathy I.* Hillsdale, NJ: The Analytic Press.

Lichtenstein, H. (1977). *The dilemma of human identity.* New York: Aronson.

Lidz, T., Fleck, S., & Cornelison, A. R. (1965). *Schizophrenia and the family.* New York: International Universities Press.

Lindemann, E. (1965). Symptomatology and management of acute grief. In H. J. Parad (Ed.), *Crisis intervention: Selected readings* (pp. 7–21). New York: Family Service Association of America.

Litowitz, B. E., & Litowitz, N. S. (1977). The influence of linguistic theory on psychoanalysis: A critical, historical survey. *International Review of Psychoanalysis, 4,* 419–448.

Litowitz, B. E., & Litowitz, N. S. (1983). The development of self-expression.

In A. Goldberg (Ed.), *The future of psychoanalysis* (pp. 397–427). New York: International Universities Press.

Loewald, H. W. (1960). On the therapeutic action of psychoanalysis. In *Papers on psychoanalysis* (pp. 221–256). New Haven, CT: Yale University Press, 1980.

Loewald, H. W. (1962). Superego and time. In *Papers on psychoanalysis* (pp. 33–52). New Haven, CT: Yale University Press, 1980.

Loewald, H. W. (1973). On internalization. In *Papers on psychoanalysis* (pp. 69–86). New Haven, CT: Yale University Press, 1980.

Loewald, H. W. (1975). Psychoanalysis as an art and the fantasy character of the psychoanalytic situation. In *Papers on psychoanalysis* (pp. 352–371). New Haven, CT: Yale University Press, 1980.

Loewald, H. W. (1976). Perspectives on memory. In *Papers on psychoanalysis* (pp. 148–173). New Haven, CT: Yale University Press, 1980.

Loewald, H. W. (1980a). Ego-organization and defense. In *Papers on psychoanalysis* (pp. 174–177). New Haven, CT: Yale University Press, 1980.

Loewald, H. W. (1980b). The experience of time. In *Papers on psychoanalysis* (pp. 138–147). New Haven, CT: Yale University Press, 1980.

Loewald, H. W. (1980c). *Papers on psychoanalysis*. New Haven, CT: Yale University Press, 1980.

Lukes, C. A., & Land, H. (1990). Biculturality and homosexuality. *Social Work, 35*, 155–161.

Mahler, M. S., Pine, F., & Bergman, A. (1975). *The psychological birth of the human infant*. New York: Basic Books.

Mancuso, J. E., & Sarbin, T. R. (1983). The self-narrative in the enactment of roles. In T. R. Sarbin & K. E. Scheibe (Eds.), *Studies in social identity* (pp. 233–253). New York: Praeger.

Mandler, J. M. (1984). *Stories, scripts and scenes: Aspects of schema theory*. Hillsdale, NJ: Erlbaum.

Mandler, J. M. (1990). A new perspective on cognitive development in infancy. *American Scientist, 78*, 236–243.

Margolen, M. H., & Goldman, S. (1974). Beyond reinforcement: Integrating relationship and behavior therapy. *Clinical Social Work Journal, 2*(2), 96–104.

Mead, G. H. (1934). *Mind, self and society* (Compiled by C. Morris). Chicago: University of Chicago Press.

Meissner, W. W. (1981). Internalization in psychoanalysis. [Monograph 50]. *Psychological Issues, 13*(2). New York: International Universities Press.

Meyer, A. (1957). *Psychobiology: A science of man*. Springfield, IL: Thomas.

Mink, L. O. (1978). Narrative form as a cognitive instrument. In R. H. Canary & H. Kozicki (Eds.), *The writing of history: Literary form and historical understanding* (pp. 129–149). Madison: University of Wisconsin Press.

Mishler, E. G. (1979). Meaning in context: Is there any other kind? *Harvard Educational Review, 49,* 1–19.

Mitchell, S. A. (1988). *Relational concepts in psychoanalysis: An integration.* Cambridge, MA: Harvard University Press.

Modell, A. H. (1988). The centrality of the psychoanalytic setting and the changing aims of treatment. *Psychoanalytic Quarterly, 57,* 577–596.

Modell, A. H. (1990). *Other times, other realities: Toward a theory of psychoanalytic treatment.* Cambridge, MA: Harvard University Press.

Nelson, K. (1985). *Making sense: The acquisition of shared meaning.* New York: Academic Press.

Nelson, K. (Ed.). (1986). *Event knowledge: Structure and function in development.* Hillsdale, NJ: Erlbaum.

Nelson, K. (1989a). The linguistic construction of self in time. In K. Nelson (Ed.), *Narratives from the crib* (pp. 284–308). Cambridge, MA: Harvard University Press.

Nelson, K. (1989b). Monologue as representation of real-life experience. In K. Nelson (Ed.), *Narratives from the crib* (pp. 27–72). Cambridge, MA: Harvard University Press.

Nelson, K. (Ed.). (1989c). *Narratives from the crib.* Cambridge, MA: Harvard University Press.

Novey, S. (1968). *The second look: The reconstruction of personal history in psychiatry and psychoanalysis.* Baltimore: Johns Hopkins University Press.

Ogden, T. (1982). *Projective identification and psychotherapeutic technique.* New York: Aronson.

Ong, W. J. (1982). Oral remembering and narrative structures. In D. Tannen (Ed.), *Analyzing discourse: Text and talk* (pp. 12–24). Washington, DC: Georgetown University Press.

Palombo, J. (1987). Critique of Schamess' concept of boundaries. *Clinical Social Work Journal, 15,* 284–293.

Palombo, J. (1989, March). *Current developments in self psychology.* Paper presented to Psychodynamic Educators in Social Work at Loyola University, Chicago.

Palombo, J. (1989, November). *Bridging the chasm between developmental theory and clinical theory.* Paper presented at the Second National Clinical Conference of the Committee on Psychoanalysis of the National Federation of Societies of Clinical Social Work, Philadelphia.

Parsons, T. (1964). *Social structure and personality.* New York: The Free Press.

Perlman, H. H. (1979). *Relationship: The heart of helping people.* Chicago: University of Chicago Press.

Piaget, J. (1962). *Play, dreams and imitation in childhood.* New York: Norton.

Polanyi, L. (1979). So what's the point? *Semiotica, 25,* 207–241.

Polanyi, M., & Prosch, H. (1975). *Meaning.* Chicago: University of Chicago Press.

Polkington, D. E. (1988). *Narrative knowing and the human sciences.* Albany: State University of New York Press.

Racker, H. (1968). *Transference and countertransference.* New York: International Universities Press.

Rapaport, D. (1951). *The organization and pathology of thought.* New York: Columbia University Press.

Reiser, M. F. (1984). *Mind, brain, body.* New York: Basic Books.

Richmond, M. E. (1917). *Social diagnosis.* New York: Russell Sage Foundation.

Robbins, F. P., & Sadow, L. A. (1974). A developmental hypothesis of reality-processing. *Journal of the American Psychoanalytic Association, 22,* 344–363.

Robinson, J. A. (1981). Personal narratives reconsidered. *Journal of American Folklore, 94,* 58–85.

Rothenberg, A. (1988). *The creative process of psychotherapy.* New York: Norton.

Rubenstein, R., & Lasswell, H. D. (1966). *The sharing of power in a psychiatric hospital.* New Haven, CT: Yale University Press.

Rycroft, C. (1956). Symbolism and its relationship to the primary and secondary process. *International Journal of Psychoanalysis, 37,* 137–146.

Saari, C. (1976). Affective symbolization in the dynamics of character disordered functioning. *Smith College Studies in Social Work, 46,* 79–113.

Saari, C. (1986). *Clinical social work treatment: How does it work?* New York: Gardner Press.

Saari, C. (1988). Interpretation: Event or process. *Clinical Social Work Journal, 16,* 378–389.

Sanville, J. (1987). Creativity and the constructing of self. *The Psychoanalytic Review, 74,* 263–279.

Sarbin, T. R., & Scheibe, K. E. (1983). A model of social identity. In T. R. Sarbin & K. E. Scheibe (Eds.), *Studies in social identity* (pp. 5–28). New York: Praeger.

Schafer, R. (1968). *Aspects of internalization.* New York: International Universities Press.

Schafer, R. (1976). *A new language for psychoanalysis.* New Haven, CT: Yale University Press.

Schafer, R. (1980). Narration in the psychoanalytic dialogue. *Critical Inquiry, 7,* 29–53.

Schafer, R. (1983). *The analytic attitude.* New York: Basic Books.

Schimek, J. G. (1975). A critical reexamination of Freud's concept of unconscious mental representation. *International Review of Psychoanalysis, 2*(1), 171–187.

Schwaber, E. (1981). Empathy: A mode of analytic listening. *Psychoanalytic Inquiry, 1,* 201–213.

Schwartz, A., & Goldiamond, I. (1975). *Social casework: A behavioral approach.* New York: Columbia University Press.

Scott, D. (1990). Practice wisdom: The neglected source of practice research. *Social Work, 35,* 564–568.

Searles, H. F. (1979). Dual- and multiple-identity processes in borderline ego functioning. In *Countertransference and related subjects: Selected papers* (pp. 460–478). New York: International Universities Press.

Seton, P. (1981). Affect and issues of separation–individuation. *Smith College Studies in Social Work, 52*(1), 1–11.

Shank, R. C., & Abelson, R. P. (1977). *Scripts, plans, goals and understanding.* Hillsdale, NJ: Erlbaum.

Shotter, J. (1989). Social accountability and the construction of 'you'. In J. Shotter & K. J. Gergen (Eds.), *Tests of identity* (pp. 133–151). London: Sage.

Siegelman, E. Y. (1990). *Metaphor and meaning in psychotherapy.* New York: Guilford Press.

Singer, M. T. (1965). Thought disorder and family relations of schizophrenics: IV. Results and implications. *Archives of General Psychiatry, 12,* 201–212.

Spence, D. P. (1982). *Narrative truth and historical truth: Meaning and interpretation in psychoanalysis.* New York: Norton.

Spitz, R. (1965). *The first year of life.* New York: International Universities Press.

Sroufe, L. A. (1989). Relationships, self, and individual adaptation. In A. J. Sameroff & R. N. Emde (Eds.), *Relationship disturbances in early childhood: A developmental approach* (pp. 70–94). New York: Basic Books.

Stern, D. (1985). *The interpersonal world of the infant.* New York: Basic Books.

Stern, D. (1989a). The representation of relational patterns: Developmental considerations. In A. J. Sameroff & R. N. Emde (Eds.), *Relationship disturbances in early childhood: A developmental approach* (pp. 52–69). New York: Basic Books.

Stern, D. N. (1989b). Crib monologues from a psychoanalytic perspective. In K. Nelson (Ed.), *Narratives from the crib* (pp. 309–319). Cambridge, MA: Harvard University Press.

Stolorow, R. D. (1988). Transference and the therapeutic process. *Psychoanalytic Review, 75,* 245–253.

Stolorow, R. D., Brandshaft, B., & Atwood, G. (1987). *Psychoanalytic treatment.* Hillsdale, NJ: The Analytic Press.

Stonequist, E. V. (1937). *The marginal man.* New York: Scribner.

Sullivan, H. S. (1953). *The interpersonal theory of psychiatry. Collected works* (Vol. I). New York: Norton.

Thorndyke, P. (1977). Cognitive structures in comprehension and memory of narrative discourse. *Cognitive Psychology, 9,* 77–110.

Tiefer, L. (1987). Social constructionism and the study of human sexuality. In P. Shaver & C. Hendrick (Eds.), *Sex and gender* (pp. 70–94). Newbury Park, CA: Sage Publications.

Tomkins, S. S. (1963). *Affect, imagery and consciousness.* New York: Springer.

von Bertalanffy, L. (1968). *General system theory: Foundations, development, applications.* New York: Braziller.

Vygotsky, L. S. (1962). *Thought and language.* Cambridge, MA: M.I.T. Press.

Watson, J. B. (1919). *Psychology from the standpoint of behaviorist.* Philadelphia: Lippincott.

Watson, R. (1989). Monologue, dialogue and regulation. In K. Nelson (Ed.), *Narratives from the crib* (pp. 263–283). Cambridge, MA: Harvard University Press.

Watzlawick, P. (Ed.). (1984). *The invented reality.* New York: Norton.

Werner, H. (1978). The concept of development from a comparative and organismic point of view. In S. S. Barton & M. B. Franklin (Eds.), *Developmental processes: Heinz Werner's selected writings* (Vol. 1, pp. 107–130). New York: International Universities Press.

Werner, H., & Kaplan, B. (1963). *Symbol formation.* New York: Wiley.

White, H. (1980). The value of narrativity in the representation of reality. *Critical Inquiry, 7,* 5–30.

White, R. W. (1963). Ego and reality in psychoanalytic theory. [Monograph 2]. *Psychological Issues, 3*(2).

Whorf, B. L. (1971). *Language, thought and reality.* Cambridge, MA: The M.I.T. Press.

Winnicott, D. W. (1947). Hate in the countertransference. In *Collected Papers: Through paediatrics to psychoanalysis* (pp. 194–203). New York: Basic Books, 1958.

Winnicott, D. W. (1956). Paediatrics and childhood neurosis. In *Collected Papers: Through paediatrics to psychoanalysis* (pp. 316–321). New York: Basic Books, 1958.

Winnicott, D. W. (1958a). The capacity to be alone. In M. M. R. Khan (Ed.), *The maturational processes and the facilitating environment* (pp. 29–36). New York: International Universities Press, 1965.

Winnicott, D. W. (1958b). *Collected Papers: Through paediatrics to psychoanalysis.* New York: Basic Books.

Winnicott, D. W. (1960). Ego distortion in terms of true and false self.. In M. M. R. Khan (Ed.), *The maturational processes and the facilitating environment* (pp. 140–152). New York: International Universities Press, 1965.

Winnicott, D. W. (1965). *The maturational processes and the facilitating environment: Studies in the theory of emotional development.* New York: International Universities Press.

Woods, M. E., & Hollis, F. (1990). *Casework: A psychosocial therapy.* New York: Random House.

Zaniardi, C. (1990). Introduction. In C. Zaniardi (Ed.), *Essential papers on the psychology of women* (pp. 1–38). New York: New York University Press.

Zetzel, E. (1970). *The capacity for emotional growth.* New York: International Universities Press.

Index

Abelson, R. P., 66
Abusive relationships
  and borderline functioning, 111, 113
  sexual abuse in. *See* Sexual abuse
Acculturation of immigrant groups, 53
Achievement
  of future goals
    ability to imagine, 174–175
    narratives on past experiences affect-
      ing, 156, 160, 164
  of generativity, 86
Acting out of past difficulties, 172
Action patterns
  and event representations, 69, 106
  inherited, 22
  and memory, 63, 171, 172
Adaptive behavior, 41
  collaboration in, 47, 48
  in evaluation of safety, 28
  in mental health, 4, 43, 44–47
  as therapeutic aim, 45
Adolescents
  identity in, 30
  persistent denial in, 85
Affect, 27–28, 78–79
  attunement, 23–24
  in client–therapist relationship, 127,
    128, 135, 161, 175
  communication through, 23, 26
  creating new consciousness, 175
  deficits in experience of, and border-
    line functioning, 113
  and inner life, 28
  in mother–child interactions, 23
  and transcontexting, 175
  categorical, 23, 26, 27, 76
  in children and infants, 27
  and cognition, 21, 25, 37

in evaluation of current state of self,
    129, 130
  in therapeutic relationship, 120
communication of, 25
intensity of, 27, 81
regulatory function of, 76
and sense of organization, 26–27
tolerance, 27, 79, 81, 82
  in borderline functioning, 109
  in character-disordered functioning,
    102, 126, 150, 151
  in ideal functioning of operational
    self, 93
  in narcissistic functioning, 114
  in psychotic functioning, 96
vitality, 23, 128, 175
Affiliation need, 6
Agar, M., 144
Age. *See also* Children and infants
  and sense of self, 23
  and use of categorical systems, 68
Aggression, 6
Ainsworth, M. D. S., 77
Allen, V. L., 54
Ambivalence
  in child–caretaker relationship,
    40–41
  in client–therapist relationship, 131
Amodal perception, 65–66
Anger, 26
  and interpsychic space in treatment,
    128
  regulatory function of, 76
  sense of self in, 79
Annihilation threat, 59, 87
  in psychotic functioning, 147
Anorexia nervosa, 22
Anxiety, adaptive purpose of, 28

201